POSTINDIAN CONVERSATIONS

ARL:

Postindian Conversations

Gerald Vizenor and A. Robert Lee

UNIVERSITY OF NEBRASKA PRESS : LINCOLN AND LONDON

Publication of this volume was assisted by The
Virginia Faulkner Fund, established in memory of
Virginia Faulkner, editor-in-chief of the University
of Nebraska Press.

Library of Congress Cataloging in Publication Data
Vizenor, Gerald Robert, 1934–
Postindian conversations / Gerald Vizenor and
A. Robert Lee.   p.   cm. – (American Indian lives)
Includes bibliographical references.
ISBN 0-8032-4666-8 cloth : alkaline paper
1. Vizenor, Gerald Robert, 1934–   – Interviews.
2. Authors, American – 20th century – Interviews.
3. Indians of North America – Mixed descent –
Interviews.   4. Indian authors – United States –
Interviews.   5. Indians in literature.   I. Lee, A.
Robert, 1941–   .   II. Title.   III. Series.
PS3572.I9Z47 1999   813'.54–dc21   99-11411 CIP

For Laura Jane Hall and Josefa Vivancos-Hernández

Contents

POSTINDIAN CONVERSATIONS

A. ROBERT LEE

Introduction

Crossbloods are a postmodern tribal bloodline.

"Crossbloods," in *Crossbloods: Bone Courts, Bingo, and Other Reports* (1976, 1990)

I was a crossblood on the natural margins of a
cultural contradance.

"Envoy to Haiku," in *Interior Landscapes: Autobiographical Myths and Metaphors* (1990)

The Indian became the other of manifest manners,
the absence of real tribes, the inventions in the
literature of dominance.

"Double Others," in *Manifest Manners: Postindian Warriors of Survivance* (1994)

The *indian* is a simulation, the absence of natives;
the *indian* transposes the real, and the simulation
of the real has no referent, memory, or native stories.
The *postindian* must waver over the aesthetic ruins
of *indian* simulations.

Fugitive Poses: Native American Indian Scenes of Absence and Presence (1998)

MUCH AS THEY TURN UPON America's Native legacy, the conversations that make up this volume can claim a quite truly
international birthing.

On the one hand, they highlight the views of Gerald Vizenor
as leading Native American novelist, poet, and essayist; enrolled
Anishinaabe (or Chippewa-Ojibway) member of Minnesota's
White Earth Reservation; currently a professor at the University
of California, Berkeley, whose life and voluminous interests and
writings have as frequently led him across Europe and Asia as
America.

On the other hand, Vizenor's interlocutor is a British scholar
of American culture with an academic berth for more than two
decades in the medieval city of Canterbury, a frequent visiting teacher to American campuses from Princeton to Berkeley,

by transatlantic chance the almost-sharer of a name with the Confederacy's general in chief, and currently the holder of a professorship at Nihon Daigaku, Tokyo's largest university.

Our exchanges, moreover, since their first tapings in Berkeley, have several times been reworked in locales that add Hong Kong, Macau, Minnesota, and South Dakota to those of California, Kent, and Tokyo. What could be more fitting, given Gerald Vizenor as literary all-rounder whose storytelling readily, though always transformingly, spans Tianjin in China, the municipal zoo in Oakland, Chaco Canyon in New Mexico, and White Earth itself, with the headwaters of the Mississippi to its north; whose essays on Native-white encounter uninhibitedly cross time from the Columbian landfall in 1492 to Wounded Knee in 1890 to the rise of contemporary tribal casinos; and who has been not only among the most traveled but simply the most prolific of all Native authors?

Japan also affords a quite especial link. As a young army private in the 1950s Vizenor found himself doing military service at Camp Chitose on Hokkaido, the country's northernmost island, and later at a post in Sendai. It was there, at nearby Matsushima, that he first encountered the haiku of Matsuo Basho, a form of poetry he himself has gone on to write often, and which became part of the classes he took in Asian studies as a student at the University of Minnesota. His own collected haiku poems would appear as *Matsushima: Pine Islands* (1984), with a recent compilation, *Cranes Arise: Haiku Scenes* (1998), just completed. He has also several times spoken of passing fantasies in which he became a kind of transposed Native American Lafcadio Hearn, acting out his own fused Euro-American-Anishinaabe-Asian mask in a culture itself famously given over to mask, whether in the form of kabuki, bunraku, noh, or the tea ceremony. From the start, thus, and symptomatically, the Japan he first saw in 1953 has embroiled him as much in imagination as in life.

This, too, would be a process for almost all the history that went into his making. For however else Vizenor is to be thought – city-raised Minneapolis crossblood, army enlistee, onetime staff writer on the *Minneapolis Tribune*, hands-on inner-city community activist, professor of Native and American studies – he has assuredly been one of Native America's literary stalwarts ("storier," in his own term). Across every kind of genre, haiku to be sure but also other poetry, his half-dozen novels, the several essay collections, the story cycles, his full-length polemical work, an anthology of Native writings, a film and stage work, and a landmark autobiography, he has put into view, and into textual play and challenge, a rare, spirited, and often cheeringly sexual panorama of fabulation as to what, and what not, it has been both to inherit and to live inside Native American identity.

Anyone entering Vizenor's textual world, with its speakerly trickster ironies, will also quickly enough accommodate to its equally writerly vocabulary, such as *postindian, crossblood, mixedblood, shadow distance, fugitive poses, double others, invented indians, sovenance,* and *survivance*. These and a gallery of others bear the signature of a writer whose voice from the start has been endemically playful yet unflinching; full of tease yet at the same time seriously unwilling to settle for any or all of the essentialist versions of Native history and identity.

How otherwise, he has argued, best to understand the contradictory skeins whereby "Indians" have been at once represented and at the same time breathtakingly un- or misrepresented throughout all the contrary turns of American culture? In this regard he has especially born down upon "savagism," be it of Rousseau's noble variety or Caliban-devilish (Cotton Mather's *The Wonders of the Invisible World* [1693] spoke early of Massachusetts's Native lands as "the devil's territories"), or be it in the updates of the "firewater" myths whereby Native peoples become somehow America's unique abusers of alcohol. This, for Vizenor, resurfaced in the late Michael Dorris's *The Broken Cord* (1989), the deeply affecting story of his single-parent adoption of Adam, a tribal boy with Fetal Alcohol Syndrome, yet troubling in how Dorris (with his wife, Louise Erdrich) spoke of court-ordered abortion and imprisonment for Native alcoholic mothers.

His gaze, however, has lowered even more upon each Euro-American projection of "the Indian." One focus would be literary romance figures, good and bad "Indians," from James Fenimore Cooper's Chingachgook and Chateaubriand's Atala, through Longfellow's Hiawatha and Twain's Injun Joe, to Ken Kesey's Chief Broom and J. D. Salinger's "Indian stuff" mannequins at Manhattan's Museum of Natural History as seen by Holden Caulfield in *The Catcher in the Rye* (1952). These, in all their beckoning charm or fascination, remain *imagined* "Indians," a kind of vast textual silhouette or storytelling puppetry.

Whether in fiction or otherwise, and often as he has made allusion to Native deterritorialization and massacre (be it the forced removals of the Cherokee in 1835, or the murder of Cheyenne in 1864, or the killing of Big Foot and the Minneconjou Sioux at Wounded Knee in 1890), Vizenor, moreover, has steadfastly refused to buy into the "Vanishing American" ethos. This he identifies as a mix of romanticized victimry and belief in "Indians" as fixed (heroically or otherwise) first into a frontier or wilderness past, then in reservations, and increasingly in the cities he calls "urban exclaves," but always, and throughout, denied anything resembling their own unabating human variousness.

Or the focus might be his analysis, with its own accompanying and deflationary wordplay, of the plethora of visualizations of "the Indian." These include Edward S. Curtis's twenty volumes of photographic stills published between 1907 and 1930 ("preserved metasavages"), the Cody "Wild West Shows" with Buffalo Bill as scout-hero and warpainted tribal cohorts as demon savagery, and Korczak Ziolkowski's Black Hills rock sculpture of the Lakota holy man Crazy Horse.

Film, silent or talking, supplies its own ongoing roster. Vizenor has written about, and frequently taught, D. W. Griffith's early one-reelers like *The Redman and His Child* (1908) through to a huge image-and-counterimage "Hollywood Indian" screen tradition. This, notably, looks to John Ford's *Fort Apache* (1948) and *She Wore a Yellow Ribbon* (1949), Delmer Daves's *Broken Arrow* (1950), Robert Aldrich's *Apache* (1954), John Ford's *Cheyenne Autumn* (1964), Arthur Penn's *Little Big Man* (1970), Eliot Silverstein's *A Man Called Horse* (1970), Ralph Nelson's *Soldier Blue* (1970), and latterly, a so-called revisionist Indian film like Kevin Costner's *Dances with Wolves* (1990), which, for all its use of the Sioux language and patent liberal good intent, still resorts (as Vizenor has been not alone in pointing out) to a white U.S. Cavalry hero, feathered tribespeople, an updated white-woman captivity drama, and the "Vanishing American" ethos. To these he himself would add the latest imaging of "Indians" to be found in Jonathan Wacks's *Powwow Highway* (1988) and Michael Apted's *Thunderheart* (1992) and *Incident at Oglala* (1992) – with the AIM figure of John Trudell at its center – and not least, Disney's lavish cartoon fantasy *Pocahontas* (1995).

ABC's 1949–58 *The Lone Ranger*, and its forerunner as the 1930s station WXYZ radio series, equally and inevitably has come under Vizenor's ironic purview. For just as the masked hero, played dashingly in white by Clayton Moore, and his rallying "Hi-ho Silver!" came to personify white western derring-do, so Jay Silverheels's Tonto served as "faithful Indian companion," a tribal Man Friday whose laconic monosyllables came to embody childlike "Indian talk."

It might, too, be his unyielding but as ever playfully satiric take on the continuing hold of braids-and-feather and Pocahontas "Mother Earth" stereotypes, "Indians" as boutique shamans, and lately a whole rash of TV and other self-appointed "tribal" channelers. Certainly New Age religionists, with their "Indian" crystals and other accoutrements, have had no easy time from his pen. Nor have the various museums, with their "Indian bones," artifacts, burial trophies, and like. These he places alongside coopted, and so largely unpondered, tribal place-names anglicized into, say, Connecticut or Seattle, Chicago or California; coinage like the Indian Head nickel; Pontiac and Cadillac as best-selling automobiles, with Jeep Cherokees and Winnebago motor homes in the fray; and sports teams unashamedly called the Atlanta Braves, the Cleveland Indians, the Kansas City Chiefs, or the Washington Redskins. All of these Vizenor has frequently opened to ironic scrutiny as ways in which "Indians," almost casually, and for sure dehistoricizingly, have been reduced to shadow, leftover lexical residue or cartoon.

Likewise he has made short shrift of the "wannabee" phenomenon, self-affiliating or faux "Indians" taken up with "wistful envies," as he calls them in *Fugitive Poses: Native American Indian Scenes of Absence and Presence* (1998). These, for him, found symptomatic literary voice in Forrest Carter's *The Education of Little Tree* (1976), with its paradoxically mock "true story" of a Cherokee childhood, and Jamake Highwater's *Shadow Show: An*

Autobiographical Insinuation (1986), with its "autoposer" lineages of a Blackfoot-French mother and Cherokee father.

Popular-culture incarnations are even better known, whether cowboy-and-Indian games; Boy Scout troop names; Jeff Chandler, Charles Bronson, or Richard Harris cast as "Hollywood Indians"; paratroopers with their "Geronimo" shouts; 1960s hippies in beads and body paint; or punks from New York to San Francisco, Moscow to London, in their lavish Mohawk haircuts. Vizenor might well ask: Whose "Indians" are these?

Nor does academic "Indian" anthropology, which, with its social science paradigms of kinship, totemism, and the like, has long made Native peoples both on and off the reservation into case studies, escape his hook. He has frequently teased anthropologists and their "field," whose preemptive quantifications and reified language he believes might better be termed *anthropologetics*, yet another display of what he has called in *Manifest Manners* and elsewhere "the literature of dominance."

Or it might be his shots at the notion of some pantribal, allone "Indianness." "More than a million people and hundreds of distinct tribal cultures were simulated as Indians," he writes in *Crossbloods: Bone Courts, Bingo, and Other Reports* (1990), "an invented pantribal name, one sound bears treaties, statutes, and seasons, but no tribal culture, language, religion, or landscape." Another trenchant if typically wry summary, and one that bears its own backward glance to both Columbus's entry into the New World as Spain's high admiral and to self-serving or inevitalist "white" versions of American frontierism, is to be found in his *Manifest Manners: Postindian Warriors of Survivance* (1994). There he suggests that "the Indian was an occidental invention; the word has no referent in tribal languages."

Given an indigenous America, or indeed Americas, so ancestral and yet, against whatever odds, so continuingly peopled, and whether by the founding Olmecs, Mayans, and Aztecs, or by each myriad native clan and grouping, whether his own Chippewa-Ojibways, the Algonquin confederation, the Navajos, Laguna and Acoma Pueblos, Sioux, Cherokees, Comanches, Arapahos, Hopis, Apaches, Osages, Zunis, Blackfeet, Salish, Chickasaws, Nez Percés, or Seminoles, and given all the burdens of these names in colonial languages, who could ever have presupposed some one composite or all-purpose "American Indian"?

Under the transforming vision of those who first sought them out, saw them for the first time, and cast them in the preemptive figures and tropes of English, Spanish, French, and other colonializing languages, they became less "Indian" than, quite exactly, "postindian" – invented or "double" others, New World chimerae, silhouettes, or shadows. The issue turns the more complex as any number of tribal people would themselves become entangled in this shifting spectacle of appearance and reality. "Indians" so have played "Indians," whether a warpath Sitting Bull, Gall, or Yellow Hand in the Cody circuses, a post-capture Geronimo parading at small-town rodeo gatherings, a Russell Means decked out as Chingachgook in the Michael Mann/Daniel Day-Lewis movie (1993) of *The Last of the Mohicans*, or a tearful Iron Eyes Cody (who once starred in Jack DeWitt's *Sitting Bull* in 1954) in buckskin and canoeing down-river against a littered industrial backdrop as part of the "Keep America Beautiful" campaign that first aired on TV in 1971.

How, by these different lights, to see, to reimagine if need be, each tribal culture as situated within its own lived time-space and calendar; or its own utterly compendious lore of Coyote and Spider Woman; or its own creation and vision myths; or its own religion of *kiva* and *katsina* and ghost, sun, and peyote cosmology; or, axially, its own sumptuous, performative oral legacy of ceremony and story? In like manner, how to elucidate and understand the cultural hybrids to follow, each Native-mainstream mix, crossover, language shift, change of geography, or generational evolution in life and consciousness?

None of this, for Vizenor, as indeed for other Native writers of his literary generation, has been to sidestep the defeats – the forced marches and removals, finagled land grabs, broken treaties or allotments – and their aftermath, in which "Indian country" like Oklahoma has played so key if largely ignominious a role. This, too, has been the history that leads into, and that helped make, contemporary Native America.

Equally there has been the vexing, enraveled issue of blood quanta. Vizenor, crossblood heir to Anishinaabe forbears, to French fur traders, and to a third-generation Swedish-American mother, has had good cause to ponder the vast concourse of *mestizos* (Spanish-Native) and *métis* (French Canadian-Native). It would indeed be hard to be true to so emphatically crossplied a history, sited and modified over time in the woodlands, reservations, and cities, and in his own case born of the lineage of urban crossblood father and a mother's midwestern Scandinavianism, and still contend that some simple *reductio* like "the Indian" could ever come even close to fitting the bill.

And quite as controversially Vizenor has also directed his satire the other way, most notably in his dismay at some of the leadership of the American Indian Movement (AIM), as embodied in the person of Dennis Banks especially, whose purposes he has taken to serve more self-interest than the interests of the different tribal and urban mixedblood communities. Literature quite literally stepped into life when his *Minneapolis Tribune* reports on the way Banks's drugs and showmanship entered the 1970s Wounded Knee and other memorial celebrations ("kitschyman" and "revolutionary tribal caravan" have been among his phrasings) showed anything but due, admiring piety. Quite "untribally," Vizenor was threatened with death.

In these respects, and not least in terms of his own cultural eclecticism, if he has sought to counter stereotype by deploying tribal lore like the great Anishinaabe trickster figure of Naanabozho, or by quite singular retellings of bear, raven, or crow animism, or by his respect for a lived tribal shamanism, so too has he availed himself freely of contemporary and assuredly postmodern theories of representation from Barthes to Jabès, Foucault to Lyotard – with Baudrillard's deployments of the ways of simulation and dissimulation as explored in *Simulacra and Simulation* (1994) an especially strong contributing influence.

The upshot, throughout his writings, and whether in his fantastical plotlines, Elizabethan plenitude of characters and namings, speculative essays, and each flighted word invention, has been a kind of tribal-cum-postmodern riposte. This takes the form of an ongoing critique imbued, as always, with keenest historical awareness (as born out in the very title of *Manifest Manners: Postindian Warriors of Survivance*), yet given over to his own uniquely postmodern, or more to the point his own uniquely postindian, styling.

Postindian Conversations offers a conspectus, a body of wide-ranging commentary that if derived from an initially agreed-upon running order, has equally, throughout and almost of necessity, been open to spontaneous shifts before being revised into script. Some formalizations in reference and quotations have been necessary, but, neither of us would hope, not at the expense of the live exchange, the speaking voice. The upshot, too, leaves little to doubt that if these exchanges explore the range as much as the acuity of Vizenor's own vantage point, they do so again, and throughout, as imbued by his long personal intimacy with the many (and often competing) discourses of Native experience.

Nor does it take long to see that though his forays into the contradictions of Native presence in "these United States" take few prisoners, they rarely do so at the expense of an inveterate comic-trickster irony. For however little a respecter of any one or another piety, Native along with non-Native, Vizenor has invariably brought to bear geniality, the companionable touch (many would say the flourish) of his own several and ongoing styles of baroque.

How, then, yet more precisely, to set these conversations in the overall context of Gerald Vizenor's life and authorship?

One evident point of departure lies in his *Interior Landscapes* (1990). There, in twenty-nine "autobiographical myths and metaphors," each dated yet gapped one from another, Vizenor unravels a helix of his own pasts. Few would doubt that this "crossblood remembrance" offers an imaginative tour de force, a circle or interlinking round of life panels that spans Minneapolis to White Earth to Japan to Berkeley. They also forswear simple narrative sequence in favor of the one story told inside, or in apposition with, the other. *Interior Landscapes* has justly been compared to advantage with Scott Momaday's wonderfully lyric Kiowa, Jemez Pueblo, and Navajo self-telling in *The Names* (1976) and Leslie Marmon Silko's Laguna Pueblo memory-and-image portraiture in *Storyteller* (1981).

The opening full-page, black-and-white photograph in *Interior Landscapes* offers "Clement Vizenor and son Gerald, in Minneapolis, 1936." (Some of the biography that follows reworks material that first appeared in my introduction to *Shadow Distance: A Gerald Vizenor Reader*, 1994.) As an image of parent-child affection it looks replete. Smiling, open-shirted, a father in fedora holds his two-year-old in protective arms. The boy, bright-eyed, wrapped, although the "subject" of the camera, appears to be monitoring its very action. Behind them lie piled-up bricks and two stern, crumbling houses, one with a curtained window. The picture contains more than a few dark hints of prophecy.

First, Clement William Vizenor, a "reservation mixedblood in dark clothes," a Chippewa house painter and feckless ladies' man, within a year would be found murdered with his throat cut in another Minneapolis street. Police left the death as "unsolved," the consequence of a robbery perhaps or a jilted husband's revenge – at any rate, that of another "Indian" who had got himself killed. Fatherless, his son would be quickly deposited with relatives, or fostered out, by his unavailing yet three-times married mother, Laverne Lydia Peterson. It was a passed-around young life and anything but well served.

In 1950, resentful at high school, denied a coherent family life by death and abandonment, and in spirit if not in reality a dropout, the fifteen-year-old Vizenor lied about his age and entered the Minnesota National Guard. This, too, was the ex–Boy Scout who had been sent to camp on onetime Anishinaabe tribal grounds. In October 1952, when he turned eighteen, he enlisted in the army, did his training in Fort Knox, Kentucky, and by spring 1953 found himself on a troopship that, en route to Korea, would deposit him in Japan. From there he variously became tank commander, scriptwriter, and jack-of-all-trades in an entertainment unit, an army serviceman in civilian clothes whose love affair with Aiko Okada took him to Matsushima and other coastal venues; from Japan he stepped back first to Washington DC, thinking to become a media specialist, and then to New York City, where during 1955–56 he became a full-time student at New York University.

But cash was short, and from 1956 to 1960 he transferred to the University of Minnesota, majoring in child development and Asian studies. On graduation he married Judith Horns (they divorced in 1969), and in honor of the birth of their son, Robert Vizenor, he produced *Born in the Wind*, ten celebratory poems, to be followed in 1962 with *Two Wings the Butterfly: Haiku Poems in English*. After social work in the Minnesota State Reformatory he returned between 1962 and 1964 to the university for graduate studies, then, from 1964 to 1968, stepped into politics, and much local controversy, as director of the American Indian Employment Center in Minneapolis.

His essays on James White Hawk, a mixedblood Sioux sentenced to life imprisonment for murder, and on Dane Michael White, a South Dakota tribal boy of thirteen who hanged himself in Wilkin County Jail, Breckenridge, Minnesota, after being left mainly in isolation for six weeks for school truancy, led him into a full-time post as reporter at the *Minneapolis Tribune*. His assignments there included a seven-part editorial series in 1973 on AIM and the whole ensuing imbroglio of Wounded Knee, the FBI, and the likes of Dennis Banks, Russell Means, and Clyde Bellecourt.

Another direction, however, beckoned when he did a year's teaching in 1970 at Lake Forest, Illinois, to be followed with an appointment in the Federal Desegregation Program in the Park Rapids School District, Minnesota; the directorship of Indian studies at Bemidji State University, Minnesota, in 1971–72; a Bush Foundation grant at Harvard in 1973; and, after his two-year stint at the *Tribune*, appointments both at Berkeley in 1976 and then the University of Minnesota in 1978.

All along, too, the literary work had been gathering pace. Through the Nodin Press (*nodin* means "wind" in Anishinaabe), he published a series of handsomely bound and printed collections including *Seventeen Chirps* (1964); *Raising the Moon Vines* (1964); *Slight Abrasions: A Dialogue in Haiku* (1966), cowritten with Jerome Downes; and *Empty Swings* (1967). Small presses such as Callimachus and Four Winds published his transcriptions of Anishinaabe tribal history, oral lore, and myth, notably *Escorts to White Earth, 1868-1968: 100 Years on a Reservation* (1968); *anishinabe adisokan: Tales of the People* (1970), the latter a revision of *Summer in the Spring* (1965, 1981, reissued 1993); *The Everlasting Sky: New Voices from the People Named the Chippewa* (1972); and *Tribal Scenes and Ceremonies* (1976), a volume made up of reprints of his journalism and magazine writing.

In the late 1970s, however, his interests drew him to novel writing, the genre that would do most to establish his reputation. *Darkness in Saint Louis Bearheart* (1978), reissued and retitled as *Bearheart: The Heirship Chronicles* in 1990, opened the account. A pilgrim's progress, at once part dream quest and part satyricon, and told as though an accidentally discovered manuscript, it gathers its journeyers into a search for the tribal Fourth World within an America as much out of spiritual balance as oil. Led by Proude Cedarfair, its Vanity Fair company passes through worlds controlled by the Evil Gambler of Anishinaabe myth, in all the reeling, irreal reality of corporate abuse, out-of-hand consumerism, "fast food fascists," and actorly counterterrorists.

In June 1983, having two years earlier married Laura Hall, a Britisher of English and Chinese-Guyanese background who had been studying at Berkeley, he left Minnesota permanently. Taking up an invitation to teach at Tianjin University, to the east of Beijing, they entered a China still, however uncertainly, under Maoist rule. In due course it led to Vizenor's second novel, *Griever: An American Monkey King in China* (1987), which weaves the "mind monkey" tricksterism of Chinese opera in the person of Sun Wu-k'ung into its Anishinaabe counterpart. Its textual gamesmanship and masked, ventriloquial hero, Griever de Hocus, give Vizenor his means to parody both communism and capitalism – the former's dire, puritanical call to party-led conformism and the latter's no-holds-barred economic profligacy.

In spring 1984, after an interlude writing in Las Cruces and Santa Fe, he returned to Berkeley, first half-time and then full-time, appointments he held for three years. In 1987 he then followed Highway 1 the seventy or so miles south to a senior professorship in literature at the University of California, Santa Cruz, becoming provost of Kresge College during 1989–90. Two years later, 1991–92 saw him in the David Burr Chair of Letters at the University of Oklahoma, Norman, before accepting his present full-time position at Berkeley. U.S. Information Service lecture and reading tours have taken him in the last decade to Canada, Japan, Germany, Italy, and Holland, interspersed with research and other trips to Britain, Scandinavia, Tanzania, Guyana, and Hong Kong.

Since the 1980s Vizenor's writings have amounted to a near flood. Each of the novels exhibits a carried-over show of canniest narrative invention, his own "tribal" storytelling, each bound into history yet, and at the same time, its own uniquely fashioned imaginative playfield.

The Trickster of Liberty: Tribal Heirs to a Wild Baronage (1988), a kind of antic detective and Berkeley-style campus novel of purloined tribal relics, anthropology, and computers, nicely exposes the gaps between academic "Indian studies" and actual historic lives. *The Heirs of Columbus* (1991) turns the Columbus saga about-face, transposing Spain's Genoese discoverer-conqueror into a returning crossblood Mayan with a descendant in Stone Columbus, above whose bingo barge, the *Santa María Casino*, is shown a laser light show of many of the main players in the story of Native America: Naanabozho, Buffalo Bill Cody, the *métis* leader Louis Riel, Crazy Horse, and Black Elk, along with Eleanor Roosevelt. Vizenor is able, thereby, simultaneously to deconstruct the Columbus lore and postindianly, as it were, to then both deinvent and reinvent the very notion of "the Indian."

In *Dead Voices: Natural Agonies in the New World* (1992), he enters Beckett terrain, a bear-woman transformation story of shamanism in the person of Bagese, set in downtown Oakland, and given the frame of the seven-card Anishinaabe chance game of *wanaki*. The novel, cannily voiced to play the oral into the written, offers one of his most challenging visions of tribal postmodernity. *Hotline Healers: An Almost Browne Novel* (1997), arguably as much story cycle as novel, places its hero, Almost, at the center of a whole "barony" of White Earth crossblood tricksters. The upshot is a pastiche of New Age and psychic phone services, the academy, a Nixon who wants "Indians" to invade Cuba, and a marvelously funny and ingenious explanation of the eighteen-minute gap in the Watergate tapes.

Vizenor's short fiction has been pitched in infinitely shared spirit. *Wordarrows: Indians and Whites in the Fur Trade* (1978, reprinted 1989), an early collection told through the persona of Clement Beaulieu in a typical piece like "Separatists behind the Blinds," which looks into Gus Hall and the Communist Party tie-up with radical movements and "Indian community" protests, works at the very shadowline of fact and fiction. Almost

Browne, in a tale named for him and in which he plies his trade in the "tribal blank book business," puts in a major early appearance in *Landfill Meditation* (1991). "Almost Browne was born on White Earth Indian Reservation. Well, he was *almost* born there . . ." runs the opening. So cagy a narrative posture puts it more squarely, or at least as equally, in the story column. The same volume, too, includes "Ice Tricksters," whose send-up of consumer "Indian sculpture" is told in appropriately trickster mock-confessional voice while offering a perfect Vizenor cameo of how "representation" has led into every kind of iconographic cul-de-sac.

Were this not scriptural plenty in its own right, Vizenor's essays, which often teasingly overlap in material with the stories, amounts to a considerable discursive archive. In *Earthdivers: Tribal Narratives on Mixed Descent* (1983) his explorations of the suicide and funeral of Dane Michael White, or of the politics of university departments of Indian studies, give a literal enough account. But they appear alongside "essays" that equally resort to a trickster cast of Mouse Proof Martin, Captain Shammer, Doc Fountain, and Father Bearald. A similar literary genre-bending holds for *Crossbloods: Bone Courts, Bingo, and Other Reports* (1976, 1990), not least in his as always companionably irreverent tilts at social science Indians in "Socioacupuncture: Mythic Reversals and the Striptease in Four Acts."

Nor should a related set of bearings be overlooked, the essay collection Vizenor edited as *Narrative Chance: Postmodern Discourse on Native American Indian Literatures* (1989), in which his introduction speaks of the "reductionism" in so much imaging of Native life and yet its own long-burgeoning literary variety – from William Apess, the Mohigan-African and Presbyterian crossblood autobiographer of *A Son of the Forest* (1829), to a generation of writers whose story talents he himself has done much to foster through his co-editorship with Louis Owens of the University of Oklahoma Press's American Indian Literature and Critical Studies Series, which includes fiction and criticism by Gordon Henry, Diane Glancy, and Lawrence Smith.

To these one would add his film *Harold of Orange* (1983), as full of trickster reversals and trompe l'oeil as anything in his fiction, and *Ishi and the Wood Ducks* (1994), in which Ishi – the lone Yahi survivor taken up in turn-of-the-century San Francisco by the anthropologist Alfred Kroeber and a figure who has long drawn Vizenor's attention – becomes an imagined colloquist in how styles of "Indian" representation have indeed evolved throughout American history. Here, too, would be postindian theater, a stage work to imitate and at the same time subvert history's own staging of "the Indian."

Vizenor, however, has now weighed in with a latest and full-length *discursus*, his *Fugitive Poses: Native American Indian Scenes of Absence and Presence* (1998). "Fugitive poses" serves perfectly as the keystone phrase, a call to attention for the great paradox of America's Native culture. If deadeningly imaged in museum displays, captivity narrative, BIA and other documentation, photography, or New Age and other bogus shamanism, Native peoples themselves, in myriad "live" ways and histories, have always confuted so static a set of reductions.

Theirs, rather, and against whatever setbacks of imposed pauperization or marginalizing, has been "transmotion," "survivance," and "performance." This amounts to a sovereignty, less of historic territory or daily politics, for all their vital importance, than of all the live, various, affirming, and ongoing dynamics of cultural practice. Vizenor so has emphasized memory, art, story, language, humor, and belief as lifeblood or plasma, the ways in which imagination gives – and, in its powers both to remember and create and recreate, sustains – an evolving Native identity.

Fugitive Poses offers Vizenor at strength, a fierce, eclectically detailed anatomy of the "theaters" of contradiction that have held sway both about and within Native life and culture. "This misrecognition of natives as *indians* is both oppressive and a prison of false identities," he says in "Tragic Wisdom," his shrewdly entitled prologue. An observation angled as may be to the interests of a book that was the foundation for addresses given in the name of the Great Emancipator, the Abraham Lincoln Lecture Series of 1998 at the University of Nebraska, it affords an equally apt point of departure to *Postindian Conversations*.

Postindian Conversations falls into what it is hoped will be seen as the unfolding sequence (no doubt unsequence) of Vizenor's life and art. "Postindian Memories" opens proceedings with the principal contours of Vizenor's life from child to adult, Minnesota to Japan, Bemidji State to Berkeley, along with his ample and ongoing asides. "Autobiographies" revisits the remembered worlds set forth in *Interior Landscapes*, above all the great play of chance, or happenstance, in his personal history. "Haiku Scenes" evokes Japan, an Asia for him indeed both literal and imagined, along with the remembrance of his own early call not only to poetry but to his other styles of authorship. "Scripts and Plays" then take up his ventures into film and theater as refracted in *Harold of Orange* and *Ishi and the Wood Ducks*.

In "Discursive Narratives" the keynote term "postindian" is given full amplification, Vizenor in polemical mode, the thinker-writer as controversialist. Here the focus turns to the always vexed, disputatious issues of "Indian" representation, the competitions of myth or stereotype with history. Columbus, inevitably, enters the reckoning, whether as High Renaissance saint or colonialist scourge or, on a vintage contrary note, actually neither.

"Bearheart Chronicles" takes up Vizenor's novel writing, his first full-length visionary story as both high invention in its own right – a latter-day anatomy of American consumer obsessions and appetite – and a prelude to the career to follow. "Griever in China" ponders, or rather re-ponders, the trickster-abroad life that was both his own journey to Tianjin and then became the mythy, priapic tale of a White Earth tribal monkey king set loose in a state-run and puritanical People's Republic of China. "Tricksters of Liberty," in turn, bears upon both the novel of the same name and *The Heirs of Columbus*, two metafictions on the ways "Indians" have both been taken over by, and yet at the same time quite eluded, American historical consciousness.

"Games of Dead Voices" speaks to Vizenor's conception, and framing and telling, of *Dead Voices*, his Oakland-set novel as at once a vision of Native life in the city and yet of a far older bear shamanism. In "Almost Browne Stories" the focus is Vizenor's latest story cycle, Almost as perhaps his most consummate trickster protagonist at work (and play) both in the "barony" of White Earth and beyond.

"Visionary Sovereignty" offers Vizenor at large, whether considering the course of his own literary life, Native political and economic self-regulation (and within that issues of land rights and Native-run casinos), tribal "leadership," Native feminism, or the future of Native culture, identity, and studies in an America newly, millenially, awakened to the challenges and cultural politics of its own ever-burgeoning multiculturalism.

Neither of the co-makers of this book would wish to be thought in any haste to conclude: Native America itself, in all its varying peoples, timelines, locales, memories, and storyings, serves as a prompt to greatest caution against the easy shot or synopsis. But that is not to inhibit a full play of inquiry, the soliciting of viewpoint from a leading Native writer whose contributions in word and art have been as undeniable as they have been plentiful.

Storyteller, maker of "wordarrows" in another phrase of his own devising, and as conscious of his personal Anishinaabe legacy in dream song and tricksterism as of a Euro-American modernity and its implications for Native America, Vizenor has been a major player in the century's efflorescence of Native literary word. This, as he well knows, and has often and readily celebrated, among others embraces D'Arcy McNickle (Cree/Salish), N. Scott Momaday (Kiowa), Leslie Marmon Silko (Laguna Pueblo), Louise Erdrich (Chippewa), James Welch (Blackfeet), Simon Ortiz (Acoma), and Louis Owens (Choctaw). But it in no way lessens or competes with their overall and several achievements to call attention to what has been so singular about his writings.

For as these conversations bear out, and not least for a colloquist from across the Atlantic, who more than Gerald Vizenor can be said to have given timelier postindian guidance to postindian times?

1

Postindian Memories

A. ROBERT LEE: Gerald, could we begin our conversations with a question about your childhood? What now persists in your memories of childhood?

GERALD VIZENOR: Stories, and the constant tease of humor. I mean the good stories of my families and friends, not the manifest manners of storybooks.

ARL: More than any other memory?

GV: Yes, the humor in the stories. But memory is tricky. Memory is a tease, an eternal tease, and always more than one story. Maybe most memories are visual – mine are – and that creates a sense of motion and a choice of stories, or points of view, as memories turn in stories.

ARL: What, then, is the "eternal tease"?

GV: Memory is my chance, nature is chance, so the eternal tease is chance, and we are much wiser by nature and chance than by traditions and terminal creeds.

ARL: How are your stories a tease?

GV: Robert, think about the tease of a nickname, the visual scene that creates the nickname, and the many stories that turn on that name. So, are the memories of names a natural tease, or the ironic creation of a presence in stories? Maybe my memories are the creation of my chancy presence. Maybe my memories precede me, the very tease of creation, and my stories are the ransom of a presence. Maybe not, but only those who tease memories and create stories come close enough to the ironic humor to know otherwise. Even so, the stories of our presence are the natural tease of memories, and the points of view we create must be chancy.

    I create my presence in stories, the starts, the ironies, pleasures, and humor of my very being in the word, right there in the text that lives beyond my memory. I can picture humor in silence, that cut of seasons, the hunt of shadows, and even see the absence, but fear is not the story of my life. Memory and humor are always big words, yes, and good words in the stories of our bloodline. Listen, after that meander, my thought is that memories, that visual sense of presence, and the scenes we create in stories, must outwit something. How about manners? Maybe tricky stories undo the comfy creases of tradition. The trickster is never a narrator, so in stories the trickster must tease the tragic out of piety and victimry.

ARL: What, then, is memorable at the end of trickster stories?

GV: Tricky scenes, chance conversions, and irony.

ARL: Fair enough, but let me ask you about that sense of pain and pleasure you write about in your autobiography. What comes most to your mind now about your childhood?

GV: Surely my childhood was more chance than manners, and that memory pleases me now. Even some of the most miserable situations come to mind as humor, and sometimes the memory of my grandmother and the tease of other *anishinaabe* relatives is a cue to tricky stories. So, you might ask, why didn't they take better care of me, and rescue me from fosterage? Well, stories are not a ransom. Luckily, my stories save me from the obvious, and the curse of victimry.

ARL: Say more about chance and contradictions.

GV: Consider the very chance of my conception. Lovey, my mother, told me that when she first saw my father, who was a postindian newcomer to the city, she thought he looked just like George Raft. She might not have noticed him otherwise. So my conception, and these conversations, are traced to the countenance of a movie actor. Families are chance and contradictions, and so were mine. I lived out that generous, natural ride of ambiguities, that chancy ride of the real, the many *reals*, as most people do in the world. I mean, we always seem to be on that road of choices and, at the same time, the roads of chance, and even the roads not taken.

Clement William Vizenor, my father, was *anishinaabe*, my mother was not, and we lived out a tricky introduction to post-modernity before we could ever bear the masks of modernity.

ARL: Tricky times indeed, as the after, and the later, precede the very idea of modernity. I must ask, what do you mean by post-modernity?

GV: The notion that words are wild, of course. But in a literary sense, my father, the postindian in motion to modernity, had already set back the narratives of dominance, mocked the many romantic narratives about *indians*, and cut the nasty fix of savagism and civilization, in favor of his own stories of survivance. He was already twice past a tricky reservation modernity.

Remember, my *anishinaabe* relatives started *The Progress*, the first newspaper on the White Earth Reservation, more than a century ago. Even then the editors were postindians in the sense that they were critical of federal *indian* agents and resisted the allotment act. My relatives created the first postmodern texts on the reservation, and at the same time, they brought to print the oral stories of *anishinaabe* survivance. My father was a second-generation postindian, and in the end, he took up the city.

ARL: You wrote a poem about your father, who held you in "the last photograph . . . half white, half immigrant." You wrote that "he took up the cities and lost at cards." Chance in the cities, and are you that son of a native immigrant?

GV: Yes, my father was a poker player. Naturally, he was on that tricky road to and from a modern irony, a federally recognized reservation. Alice Beaulieu, my *anishinaabe* grandmother, and my father were postindian immigrants, and in that sense postmodern natives on the move from the reservation to modernity, the industrial world of Minneapolis. So there are the contradictions, the ambiguous situations, and humor on the road to modernity. Right now, in these conversations, we are on that road of chancy, postindian memories.

ARL: By that do you mean the mythic postindian?

GV: Yes, we are mythic by conversation, conversion, and remembrance, and the pleasure is the contradiction. Natives have always been on one road of resistance or another, creating postindian myths and tricky stories in the very ruins of representation and modernity. We are postindian storiers at the curtains of that stubborn simulation of the *indian* as savage, and the *indian* as a pure and curative tradition. The *indian* is a simulation, an invention, and the name could be the last grand prize at a casino.

ARL: Could we return to the idea that fear is not your life?

GV: Listen: Dread, panic, and horror are the great teasers, and tragic wisdom is our best chance in a dangerous world. I have never lived by fear, because fear is not a life. My life, in a sense, has been a chance to outwit the panic teasers at least in stories. I was abused as a child, but not by physical violence. Not to live in the fear of violence is a chance, a chance to trust people in the ordinary sense of human confidence. I live by trust, not fear, and took the chance to trust people. Fear is real, of course, a curse of violence, and fear can be a simulation, a mundane course of separation. Fears are not my life, and neither are simulations, *indian* or otherwise.

ARL: Your autobiography uses a marvelous and greatly revealing photograph. Your father, handsome, wearing a fedora, shirt open, holds you as a baby against a rather sinister background of bricks and rubble. Even so, the scene looks idyllic. Yet within eighteen months of that photograph your father was found murdered, which required of you, in time, a self-fathering, a self-parenting. What of that childhood?

GV: There, in that photograph, his great hand on my arm, he remembers me with an eternal smile. I hear his voice at times. I remember him in my stories. You know, my father was found in an alley with his throat slashed, a postindian murdered in the city. He died, however, no more than a "halfbreed" in newspaper reports. Now, to bear my own fathering is an ironic turn of such a tragic death. I was a child, and he died so young, and now we are both the fathers of that time.

ARL: What became of your family then?

GV: Lovey, my mother, who was nineteen years old at the time, carried on by fear and loneliness. She moved away in silence. Alice, my *anishinaabe* grandmother, cared for me in that crowded apartment in downtown Minneapolis. She must have mothered me to be my own father then, and so we carried out a native sense of families. Years later, my mother tried to care for me, but after a few months she put me out to fosterage. So my fathering must be something of a sanguine critique. I had to reach out of the common course of families and create my own, to negotiate a father, a brother, a sister, and other relations over the years. And these experiences may have provided me with the natural cues of imagination, writing, and literature.

ARL: Did this context lead into the fantasy world that you created in

childhood? Was this, in classical Freudian terms, a compensa-
tion, or did it simply have its own rationale?

GV: Freudian or not, there had been a great silence. I was silent for
an entire year in the third grade of elementary school. And the
memory of my interior life then is a very pleasant thought now.
I mean, I have never thought about that year as anything but
meditative and playful. I don't remember anyone every shaming
me for my silence at the time. So the teachers pretty much left
me to myself. I attended school every day, but I never said a
word in the classroom that year. My silence then seems to make
even more sense to me now. I just stopped talking. I studied,
lived by my experiences, and remember thinking about nature
and situations near the river. I read stories then, but not many.
The Red Pony by John Steinbeck comes to mind. I created my
own language of imagination. My silence enlivened a visual
memory. I remember the pleasure of imagining *real* places. I
was not deprived by silence. Rather, my life was enriched that
year by silence. I was lucky that the teachers and social workers
left me to my silence, and they deserve praise for not crippling
my imagination with forced recitations. I was left alone to find
myself in imagination and, much later, in literature. My teacher
was generous that year because she granted me the chance of
silence, myth, and stories. Now, I suppose, my silence would be
referred to various experts and any number of state and federal
agencies. They would try to talk me out of silence and get me
back on the productive road of recitations and representations.

ARL: You've often said that you were a passed-around child. What
memory do you have of your mother in the story?

GV: Lovey lived by fear, a fateful sense of fear, and with a shy sense of
humor. She tried to care for me, but was shamed by failure and
passed me out to fosterage. I remember being moved from one
house to another, one family to another, one manner of love to
another. My fosterage was never formal, and fortunately never
the business of any state agency. My mother contracted with
several families for my care. I can tell you from my experiences
of fosterage that families are simulations. The word is a romance,
and the meaning is lost in modernity.

I witnessed violence in one of my foster families, but I was
never the subject or victim of physical violence. My memories,

for the most part, are rather pleasant. I think fondly of my mothers, fathers, brothers, and sisters of fosterage. I have no fear of these memories. I am humored by their fosterage. Much later, this humor troubled my mother. She was doubly shamed by her memories, and she could not take much pleasure in my play of personal achievements. My life had more to do with fosterage than her praise and care as a parent. Lovey, at the end of her life, was able to laugh with me about these contradictions, and she strained to be a mother in our memories.

ARL: LaVerne Peterson was a third-generation immigrant who had fallen in love with your father and, as time went on, had a very up-and-down life herself, did she not? How do you remember your mother as a presence in your life?

GV: I remember that she seldom paid her bills, which is what prompted my moves from one foster family to another. I was, in my adolescence, very critical of her neglect of me. But later, I realized that she was a high school dropout, and at the time she worked as a waitress. She was lonely, work was hard to find, and her hourly wages were very low. She could not afford to care for me or anyone, and she could not earn enough to pay the rent every month.

After my father died she left me with my grandmother for about two years, and then she insisted that we live together in a small apartment over a trunk manufacturing company in north Minneapolis. That lasted only a few months. The apartment was seldom heated, and the electricity was cut because she had not paid the bills. I was four years old and always hungry. I think her intentions were generous, but she was so lonesome as a mother. She could not survive without a man. So she put me out to fosterage.

ARL: We're talking here, more or less, about the end of the Great Depression and the start of a wartime economy in Minneapolis. Mean streets, tough times, terrible winters. Who was your father?

GV: I was too young to mourn the tragic death of my father, but he was never an absence to me. His smile and warm hands are a presence in visual memories, and yet he is a disappearance. I see a smile, and that must be his eternal tease, but there are no conversations or tricky names that bring him back in memory.

My father is my creation. Only his body is buried in an unmarked grave.

ARL: What father have you created in imagination?

GV: Well, I am *his* father now. He died at age twenty-six, and he became my son the year we were the same age. Coincidentally, the year I turned twenty-six, I reviewed for the first time the official police records and other documents about his murder. The *Minneapolis Tribune*, years later, ran a story about unsolved homicides in the city. Clement Vizenor was pictured in that story. The surname, and a similar countenance in the photograph of my father, caused many people to think that I had been murdered. You see, we were sons, brothers, and fathers on the road of postindian destiny. My father is negotiated in stories as much as memory, a touch, a family promise, and our old age.

ARL: Clement Vizenor was postindian, as you say, a crossblood on the move. Where did he grow up, and when did he move to Minneapolis?

GV: I write about this in my autobiography, *Interior Landscapes*. The nation was in a depression, and my father left the White Earth Reservation in search of work. The economy, as you might imagine, was much worse on rural reservations. He moved with his family to the city, found a job as a painter, and inspired my mother in the cast, airs, and fedora of George Raft. My mother was sixteen years old at the time. I was conceived before they were married, and born before they really got to know each other. We shared the same apartment with my *anishinaabe* grandmother, aunts, and uncles at first, and then my mother moved away after my father was murdered.

ARL: Your father was a house painter?

GV: Yes, but he didn't train for that. My father and his four brothers decided that this was the kind of work they could easily find, and they could also work together. They had enough sense to construct a family story and figure out how to paint houses as they did the work. So they worked for the same contractor and become very good painters. My father and one of his brothers were murdered at about the same time. Joseph, Lawrence, and Everett, the three surviving brothers, retired as painters in Minneapolis.

ARL: What kind of life do you suppose your father had as a young man in the city and, as it turned out, a young father in the city?

GV: My guess is that he was playing the story of a life that went way beyond what he could afford to pay. So he probably lived out the rich myth of a poor man. I doubt that he thought of himself as a mere laborer, and his gestures to women were more than those of a postindian house painter. My father wore a fedora, a tricky pose of energy. Surely his manner would have been ridiculed by some, but he was on the move, and never a signature of victimry. Likely, he saw himself as a very significant person, and a keen painter at that, who liked to gamble at poker games.

ARL: What did it mean for someone of his generation and tribal background to have moved to the city?

GV: Well, there is a distinction between his generation and mine, a radical distinction. My father comes to the city as a native from the White Earth Reservation and who cares? He certainly would not have attracted much attention as a native. My father and uncles were postindians trying to work their way into modernity. But he moved to the city during the depression, when the confidence of the nation was very weak. Workers at the time had more to worry about than the moves of *indians* in the nation. I mean, there was a twist of equality in the miseries of that economic depression, and there were no bread lines on the White Earth Reservation.

ARL: Gerald, your father seemed to have a touch of the dandy about him in that fedora. Clearly your mother lived a contingent life, skipping house, and then she put you out to various families. Can you talk more about that?

GV: LaVerne responded to the death of my father with fear, loneliness, and distance. She told me more than once that she was never at ease around my *anishinaabe* relatives. The Vizenors, she said, teased her too much, and she was insecure about her body. She was tall, and tried to hide her skinny legs, and my grandmother teased her about everything. My mother never seemed to understand that the tease, not to mention the insistence, was also an embrace. The native art of teasing embraces the obvious with intrigue and irony. The obvious truth of a tease, as my grandmother and uncles would tease, cannot be denied without more humor. My mother doubly missed the humor and embrace. She was so insecure about the obvious touch of words and that survivance humor and liberty in postindian families.

ARL: Vizenor, and cultural variations, is not a common name in any language. What is the origin, the actual story of your surname?

GV: The name was created by federal *indian* agents at the time of the first census of natives on the White Earth Reservation in Minnesota. The reservation was established in 1868. Peter Vezina, an *anishinaabe* fur trader, surely pronounced his name with an accent, and the agents transcribed what they heard as Vizenor. The origin of my name is a despotic transcription. Peter probably adopted his surname as a pay name, that is, a name he used in the fur trade because the factors in the trade were pained to record native names. And that, in part, because the *anishinaabe* might have been known by several nicknames, a common practice in native families. The *anishinaabe* fur traders were asked to choose a name that was familiar to the agents. So the story of my surname is a postindian chance that was transcribed by federal *indian* agents. The Vezina surname was related to the Vezinat families in the province of Quebec. Peter married Sophia Trotterchaud, and they lived out their lives on the White Earth Reservation.

ARL: And you have carried on in this postindian surname, except for a short period of time when your mother remarried. What of this stepfather you have written about in your autobiography?

GV: Elmer Petesch was a severe, mean man, but not at the end, not in the last year of his life. He never adopted me, but school officials assumed my surname was the same as his, and so that was my name for several years until military service. I was about eight years old when my mother married this stable, older man, and how ironic that he was a stationary engineer. The first year we lived together was my year of silence in elementary school.

Elmer was a reliable patriarch, and I had to negotiate every kind measure of attention and gesture of affection. And then, about five years into their marriage, my mother walked out on him one afternoon. Elmer came home from work and she was gone. She took up with a new man and left me with the old one, the patriarch. I could not have been a happy reminder to him, that he had been abandoned by my mother. So from that point on we had to negotiate a new relationship. Every moment was contested at first, and he slapped me around a few times, but not the kind of abuse and fear that left wounds. You smart off and you get smacked – that was a way of life then. I ran away from him several times, and after that contest, we realized that we truly needed each other. So we started our negotiations of who we were and how we would live together. We chose the metaphors of brothers rather than the troubled poses of father and son. I needed a brother more than a father, and so he became my older, troubled brother. Elmer was serious and very warm about our new relationship. We made the best of a bad situation, and we truly trusted each other in the last few months of his life.

ARL: Gerald, would you talk about his death?

GV: Elmer Petesch was born on a farm in Iowa. He seldom told stories, and none about his experiences as a farm boy. He moved to the city and became an engineer at the A. T. Rydell Company. Elmer maintained the boilers that generated power to run the millwork machines. The company was an exciting place to visit because it was truly an industrial world, a manly measure of modernity. The boilers thundered with fire, and the room was always warm. The millworkers made giant chairs to sit by the warm furnaces, and there were stacks of magazines everywhere. I loved the machines, the polished governors, pulleys, and many belts that ran between floors to power the machines, and the great scent of sawdust. These were men with humor; they teased each other, and me. Some of the workers, the younger ones, took time to show me how things worked, as they might have taught their own sons. They made precision frames and molding out of different kinds of wood. It was a rich and wonderful place. Elmer took me along many times late at night to inspect the boilers. He loved his work, and he was good to be with on the job. I would walk with him through the plant at night, among the silent machines. This company of great machines was the very place that killed a dedicated stationary engineer, and so tragically the accident happened one Christmas Eve. Elmer had agreed to work that night for a man with a young family, and as he set out alone to bank the fires in the boilers he asked me to prepare a pumpkin pie, our dessert on his return. I waited and waited, but he did not return. The doctor called me early in the morning and told me that my father had fallen in an elevator shaft. Elmer, my older brother, died in the hospital several days later.

ARL: Could we now talk about your grandmother?

GV: Alice Mary Beaulieu was born on the White Earth Reservation in 1886. Geronimo was deported as a war prisoner to Florida, and the Statue of Liberty was dedicated that same year, not that she ever noted such coincidences. At age nineteen she married Henry Vizenor. They were both *anishinaabe* and of the original families on the reservation. Sixteen years later he left his native wife and seven children and ran off with a younger woman. Henry died in Chicago. My grandmother never lost her humor, but the trouble and pain that she endured in the next few years was a test of her courage. Joseph and Truman, two of her five boys, were convicted of minor crimes and sentenced to serve one year in the Minnesota State Reformatory at Saint Cloud. Joseph, who was in love with a young white woman at the time, was convicted of carnal knowledge because she was underage. The conviction was very sad because they were young lovers and that turned out to be a crime. They were the same age, but that was not the point of the law. He was *anishinaabe* and that, no doubt, is what made their love felonious. And so he served a year in prison. Truman, my other uncle, had stolen some beer and cigarettes and was sentenced at about the same time. So the two boys served their time together in prison. Alice left the reservation during the economic depression, and after several jobs in small towns, she moved with her children to an apartment in downtown Minneapolis. There my father and his brother were murdered, and the crimes have never been solved. Truman was probably hit on the head and pushed over a railroad bridge. He drowned in the Mississippi River.

ARL: As a child were you taken regularly back to the reservation?

GV: No, never regularly. My family was never nostalgic about any reservation. They lived more by stories than by actual visits, because the reservation was a place of bad memories, abuse, corrupt traditions, and poverty. John Clement Beaulieu, my great uncle, was the one who spent the most time in reservation communities, and he brought me into that world with humor and a tricky sense of native politics. The White Earth Reservation, as you know, is a huge area, and there are many towns and treeline communities within the original treaty boundaries. I never had much contact with any community on the reservation until my college years. But at least one of my earlier visits was a chance, unintended, and that ironic story is in my autobiography. The Boy Scouts of America maintains a summer camp on the reservation, and little did I know when I took up scouting at age twelve that I would be sent back to the reservation for two weeks in the summer. I had no idea at the time because we arrived at night, the camp was remote, and the road was not familiar. I was a postindian tenderfoot from the city, the lowest rank in scouting, and the troop leaders sent me back to the reservation. The camp was rough, wild, and that irony has lasted in my memory.

ARL: Chance, as you say, and the most memorable reversals are ironic, more often than not. What about high school and your teenage years?

GV: I attended several schools in Minneapolis. Pierce, an elementary school located northeast, in an industrial part of the city, was my first institutional experience. I was with my first foster family at the time. I attended one other school before moving to Hamilton Elementary School in North Minneapolis. I finished there, including my year of silence, and moved on to the nearby Patrick Henry High School. The first couple of years were rather ordinary. I was very good at science for a year or two, but after that I could hardly bear the daily bump and scent of that institution. My interests and friends had nothing to do with school or academic life. School to me then was mostly a fraud, a deception, and a perpetual power play. Most of my friends felt the same way, but we got along, and even thrived on the absurdity. The whole ridiculous enterprise, except for a few years, bored me from beginning to end. I finally got away by enlisting in the United States Army.

My resistance, however, was not destructive. I tried to sabotage the piety of the school at every creak of authority, but never ruined property, or broke windows, or even skipped school very much. I was in the classroom most of the time, and bored to easy distraction. The outside, the seasons, and the river, were on my mind, so my inside pose was absolute academic boredom, not genius. But I was tricky and complicated and was always challenging people. One challenge, in fact, resulted in my decision to quit school in my senior year. Elmer had died the year before. I was living on my own at the time, and worried about the school social workers finding out about me. I was working part-time and had very little money, and certainly not enough to pay the cost of graduation. So I demanded an accounting of how the money was actually spent, and to avoid my challenge the social workers covered my fees with charity. I was angry, my pride compromised, and my resistance was dissolved by an anonymous ransom. I enlisted in the United States Army that autumn shortly after my eighteenth birthday.

ARL: I'm not certain about the chain of events here. You quit high school in your senior year to enlist in the army. When were you in the Minnesota National Guard?

GV: I enlisted as a private in the Minnesota National Guard at age fifteen and served for one year. I was trained to be a machine gunner at weekly sessions in the Minneapolis Armory. The Korean War started in June 1950, at the very time my unit was in summer combat training at Fort Ripley in Minnesota. A few months later our battalion was activated, and that created a problem about my age. The officers, as it turned out, knew all along that I was underage, but age was not an issue until there was a real war. They could no longer ignore my deception. I was honorably discharged after one year of service, and at the time I was only a tenth grader in high school. About a year later I enlisted in the army for three years. I completed sixteen weeks of combat infantry training at Fort Knox, Kentucky, and was destined for combat service in Korea.

ARL: You were on your way to combat service in Korea, but you ended up in Japan. How did that happen?

GV: The troopship with three thousand soldiers on board was diverted from the harbor at Inchon, on the Yellow Sea, and docked instead at Yokohama, Japan. During the next two weeks most of the soldiers boarded military flights to Korea. The flights had ended by the time they got to my name at the end of the alphabet. Japan was by the chance of my surname. I was assigned to serve in a tank battalion that had been decimated in the war, and would have returned to combat if the war had not ended that summer. My unit was stationed at Camp Chitose on Hokkaido Island. I was ordered there by chance, at the end of the alphabet. Japan by chance, and a new world of *udon*, sake, kabuki, and haiku.

ARL: Were you doing any writing at this stage?

GV: I first thought of myself as a serious writer in the military. I wrote short stories and poetry. I wrote a bit earlier, but I have no sense of it now because it was part of school assignments. I do remember, however, that my first stories were not accepted by my literature teacher because she refused to believe my experiences. One of my stories was about my time as a private in the Minnesota National Guard. She could not believe that I had completed summer combat training. This was the tenth grade, and as she looked over the classroom that autumn, over the sons and daughters of the new middle class, it's understandable that she could not bring herself to believe in me, a postindian machine gunner. I was determined to leave school and become a believable soldier and writer in Japan.

ARL: Japan was at once a military encounter for you and yet another kind of seedbed for your writing. You once thought of staying there, making a "Japanese" life?

GV: Yes, and my original plan after discharge from the military was to attend Sophia University in Tokyo. I was accepted for study, and might have become the *anishinaabe* Lafcadio Hearn. Not just by mimicry, but by romance, meditation, and the tease of cultural distance. Hearn's stories created the sounds of water, crickets, and other creatures. I had not read his books in Japan, but years later his stories touched my own memories.

        I changed my mind about staying in the country to study and, at the last minute, returned home, only to leave again for a year. I attended New York University for one year, and then continued my studies at the University of Minnesota.

        Japanese culture has been important to me since my time in the military. I was aware that my presence as a soldier, a decade after the atomic destruction of Hiroshima, the end of the Second World War, and only four years since the end of the occupation, was a reminder of defeat and a cultural distance. Not just the distance of manners and humor, but the distance of my *anishinaabe* origins and fosterage. Japanese literature, especially the haiku, touched me with a great sense of nature, memory, and impermanence. My literary life started there, in the hint of seasons, the traces of nature, and the bold court of masks. Basho's haiku poems were more accessible to me than any other literature at the time. Basho teased my nature, my sense of presence, even in translation, more brightly than the crease of sonnets by Shakespeare. Haiku was an aesthetic experience, of course, and yet the images were more emotive to me than the measure of a causal sentence. Haiku became my postindian sense of literature and, at the same time, an obscure introduction to the imagistic pleasures of *anishinaabe* dream songs.

ARL: One of the figures in literature that you took enormous pleasure in and indeed revered is Matsuo Basho. What is it about haiku that has so appealed to you?

GV: Basho is my man, a teaser of seasons, and an imagistic philosopher of impermanence. Issa is my man too, and he teased the birds and worried insects in his nature. Haiku held me to my own visual memories, not to mere tradition, and taught me that creation is in an imagistic scene. Haiku also taught me about ambiguities, and the natural impermanence of life and literature. Zen Buddhism teased the contradictions of presence as much as a water strider. Basho was a water strider. Issa was a sparrow. Buson was a crane in the mirror. I was a crane, a cedar waxwing, a bear. My presence was a creation, my own imagistic creation, and that would become my impermanence, liberation, and survivance. Basho writes about the moon over Matsushima Bay, a beautiful collection of islands, and the moon was there for me too, brightly over the pines some two centuries later. These coincidences are a literary presence.

ARL: Military service in Japan, haiku poetry, a love affair, and then you return and embarked on a college education in the United States. Why college, if you were thinking about becoming a writer?

GV: College came about by chance, and nothing more. I was discharged from the military and returned to Minnesota. I visited family and friends, and realized that I had to do something else with my life. I moved to Washington DC, rented a room, and prepared to study radio and television engineering. John Sullivan, a friend from the military, invited me to visit New York City. I arrived on the weekend and my friend said, "Listen, classes begin next week, so why don't you come along?" And so, by chance, my education started at New York University.

ARL: You studied literature for one year at New York University and then went on to the University of Minnesota. To study what?

GV: New York University was too expensive. I worked part-time at

Dell Publishing Company, and later for an automobile agency, but could never make enough money to pay my tuition. I spent my military savings and returned broke to Minnesota. Four years later I graduated with a major in child development and a minor in Asian studies. Chinese and Japanese literature became my sanctuary, and after working for a year as a social worker at the Minnesota State Reformatory, I returned to graduate study in East Asian area studies.

ARL: Who particularly steered you in this direction?

GV: Professor Edward Copeland at the University of Minnesota. He taught courses in Japanese literature, art, and culture, and he took an interest in my creative work as an undergraduate student. He encouraged me to continue graduate study, and in that way had a great influence on me at the time. Copeland had been an interpreter at the end of the war, during the military occupation in Japan. I registered in his seminar on Japanese literature in translation. This was the spring semester of my junior year, and the trees right outside the classroom window had burst into bloom. Not much was more pleasant after a long cold winter than plum blossoms on campus. The scene was a natural haiku, and that very week we were reading Basho. Copeland lectured in a gentle manner, but my interests that afternoon was outside the window. At the end of the seminar that day he left a note on my desk. The note said, "You've been looking out the window. What are you looking at?" So I wrote him a haiku poem about the tree and placed my poem on his desk at the end of the seminar the next day. I got a few blocks away from campus and was struck with insecurity. I made myself vulnerable by haiku, not a smart move in a cold institution. I had no interest in an audience, but was very worried about his response. My insecurities, of course, were completely unfounded. A few days later he responded to my poem with an original haiku of his own. What a delightful experience, a natural, pleasurable bond over a plum tree at the university. Now that was a chance, a lucky turn of images, and haiku has been on my mind ever since.

ARL: During this period you married Judith Horns and had a son, Robert. Were you also trying to write at this time?

GV: Well, there's nothing particularly original about these difficulties, juggling the pleasures and distractions of family. But it does raise that universal contradiction, the solidarity of families and, at the same time, the need to be an artist, to be solitary. The creative rush of literature is not social but singular and seclusive. Human unities are later, at publication. Albert Camus wrote a story about a painter who loved children. The more children he had, the less he painted, and he was a brilliant painter. He had worked on one painting for a long time, and then, at his death, his friends found his last work of art, a painting with a miniature word in the center of the canvas. His friends could not quite figure out if the word was *solitary* or *solidary*. The tension of creation was undecided, in a word. That story is a tease, a wistful metaphor, and my time was cornered as a writer. Robert, my son, was a delightful solidarity.

ARL: You were divorced after nine years of marriage and found yourself more and more involved in community service and activism. Housing, jobs, medical care, and human rights. How did that come about, and how did you find time to write?

GV: I was a community advocate for several years, serving natives in Minneapolis. My office was located in a settlement house at first, and then we moved to a storefront on a busy street near the urban reservation. This kind of community service, you know, the tough stand for lost, separated, sick, and hurt people, worked against my marriage. This was not an aesthetic separation of solitary or solidary, but the daily breakdown of public, private, and personal insecurities. I lived in a world of rage, the silent anger of cures and promises, and, by resistance and situational intensity, tried to change the community. Truly, there was nothing heroic to my service, because the rage came over the threshold at the center with tricky stories. Sadly, the stories were misgiving to our marriage. The tease was always there at the end of the day, but not at home, because the rage politics, the constant suspicions, surveillance, and the heartaches, were incurable troubles at the time. That trouble is with me in visual memories today.

ARL: You were working mainly with urban Indians?

GV: Some reservations, but mainly my native advocacy was on the urban reservation around Franklin Avenue in Minneapolis. There, for sure, in the early part of my community service.

ARL: What was your relationship to the people you were working with, the people on the street, and those who came to the storefront center?

GV: Street advocacy seemed natural to me at the time, in spite of the rage politics. I lived by the street as a child, many streets. There was nothing unusual about this, because these were ordinary responsibilities, the ordinary extension of my life experiences. Truly, the politics of poverty was the worst by compromise. Radical advocacy demanded more than just a good and worried heart, and street work took much more than compassion and anger. The native street demanded a strategy of rage, an antidote to curses, and clear articulation of situational ethics. I continued to write at the time, and might have lived by the imagistic grace of my haiku poems, an aesthetic scene, but the politics of the time demanded more of me. I had already published two books of haiku, *Two Wings the Butterfly* and *Raising the Moon Vines*. I had earned national attention for my original haiku. I might have lived a literary life at a different time, in another place. Haiku was a chance, a double creation of the imagistic scene, and an aesthetic literary presence. I was dealt a life of postindian rage, chance, and contradictions, and the world might have changed for my service and poems.

ARL: You're talking politics, but whose politics?

GV: The politics of racialism and dominance. But we had to make our own politics. Who would listen to the absence of politics? I started my critique of native absence and presence, dominance and survivance, during that time, but it took me more than thirty years to write about it in *Fugitive Poses: Native American Indian Scenes of Absence and Presence*. Natives are seen by their absence, as the historical presence of natives is their absence. My politics demanded a radical presence, but there were natives who resisted any change and stood by their traditions as an absence. So at the time it was important to do a number of things all at once. I have to say, however, that the politics of our circumstances was often discovered after the fact. That is, we confronted the expectations of popular culture and discovered the significance of our resistance. Ronald Libertus, George Mitchell, Bonnie Wallace, and others are the great *we* in this resistance.

ARL: This involved issues of family housing, employment, health care, police surveillance, and education?

GV: Yes, education, and the worst slumlord housing, unheated, broken windows, and higher rents for equal space elsewhere in the city. But the most critical issue at the time was health care. So, has anything changed in the past generation? The issues were clear enough then; another study only advanced the posers in the academy.

What never seems to change is the simple responsibility of finding medical care for a sick child, or training people for good jobs, or finding people a good and friendly place to live. Every day, critical situations demanded my rage, humor, and political attention as an advocate. I never had much time to study how to serve people. Just being there, at the center, in the community was enough in those days. Many serious problems came right over the threshold, and that moment was the test and meaning of situational ethics. That moment was touched by hurt, anger, doubt, uneasy trust, and survivance, and that critical moment was, at the time, the measure of our humanity. Such original moments cannot be easily studied or taught as a mere professional practice of caregivers.

I was good at the threshold, very good at situational ethics, and resisted the temptation to convert those critical moments into academic manners and the ideology of action. I can hardly bear the thought of being a witness of pain for politics and pay, and then to convert situational ethics into a testimonial salary range. The politics of hurt and anger is actual and, at the same time, a simulation, but my memories and stories of that time had to be better than venture victimry. I want much more from my memories than victimry. My stories must be as original as the situations that came over the threshold at the center. My meter is survivance, and at best, my stories are teased by an unnameable tragic wisdom. So you can understand how it pains me, doubly pains me, that moments of situational ethics are used by politicians and abused by ideologues.

ARL: So the issue becomes one of survival or, in a word you have made your own, survivance?

GV: Survivance stories honor the humor and tragic wisdom of the situation, not the market value of victimry. I am a storier of tricky scenes and tragic wisdom now, and some of that comes from my visual memories at the center. I mean, every day, almost every hour at the center, we were prepared to act, and did so in most situations. I practiced situational ethics on the streets of an urban reservation and never doubted that there would always be serious problems at the door. But at the same time, there was humor at the end of the day, always a good survivance story. Right in the middle of the most serious situations, someone would create humor, a native tease about fate and fashions. What do we name that? Downtown reservation irony? The tricky heritage of native survivance? Maybe, and do natives bear the natural wit of tragic wisdom? Not tragic victimry, but stories of survivance, and the tease of common, tragic hurts as the source of wisdom. I was an advocate, and carry every story of hurt and humor of that time in my visual memories. But, you know, service alone can also become the hand of dominance. Situations are never the same, and even native resistance is a romantic conversion of cultural dominance.

ARL: So how do natives overcome a sense of absence, even nihilism?

GV: Tricky stories are the cure. Listen, is there a wiser antidote to fear, fate, and dominance than wit, natural reason, and irony? The *anishinaabe* even tried to outwit the coldest, mundane count of winter with tricky stories. The mind, a good story, can even change the weather, and that's the start of a new season. Stories are the cure, not the pose of traditions or victimry. So Naan-abozho, that *anishinaabe* trickster and curative weather conniver, creates wild scenes, lusty situations, and outwits wicked posers, native reactionaries, and even the manners of oral traditions. The trickster assumes the natural presence of wind, stones, trees, birds, and animals, and is always in motion, a natural sense of visionary sovereignty in most native stories. The curse of absence is unbearable. Stories of survivance are a sure sense of presence. Only the silence of native stories is the end of tragic wisdom.

ARL: How would you describe your stories?

GV: Most of my stories are about survivance. No matter the miseries, most of the characters in my stories take on the world with wit, wisdom, and tricky poses. My stories are not in the tragic mode, not the themes of heroic ruin, destruction, and moral weakness. My storiers are tricky not tragic, ironic not heroic, and not the comfy representations of dominance. You can read these stories in *Dead Voices*, *Wordarrows*, and *Landfill Meditation*, and in my novels, *Griever, Bearheart, The Heirs of Columbus*, and the stories in *Hotline Healers*, and in my autobiography, *Interior Landscapes*.

ARL: Can you give me a specific example in your stories of the kind of survivance you have in mind?

GV: I wrote a story about survivance in *Wordarrows*, a scene in my visual memories that took place more than thirty years ago. I was director of that storefront service center in the native community on Franklin Avenue in Minneapolis, and was about to lock the doors one summer afternoon, at the end of the week. I was tired and ready to drive north for the weekend, out of the city. I turned to leave, and there, in the doorway, stood a native couple. The man was angular, blue, and nervous. The woman was dark, drowsy, and she wore an oversized shirt that stank of beer and vomit. The two sat in chairs near my desk. She leaned to one side and closed her eyes. Her fetid breath and sickening smell of vomit filled the small office.

The man could not wait to start his rant about racism. He blamed alcoholism and his addiction on the white man. I was moody, weary of victimry, and distracted by my own miseries, lost love, a failed marriage, and told him that some shaman might take his tribal blood back one night and solve his problems. I was angry and accused the man of self-pity. At that moment the woman raised her head and looked around my office. She seemed to smile, and then she pointed toward the doorway. "Stand now, the flag is coming through the door," she said, a reference to the native ceremonial staff of eagle feathers. Then she sang an honoring song. Her voice was strong, and this bothered the man. He warned her to stop singing. Suddenly she seemed sober, innocent, and tears ran down her face as she sang. She stood at the side of the desk and reached out to touch me with her bony, warm, and filthy fingers. She was a visionary, a healer, a withered shaman of survivance. I was moved to tears by her power, and my worries seemed to vanish that afternoon. "It feels so good to talk again," she said, and then the couple left. I never saw them again, but my stories honor their memory.

ARL: Soon after these activities you became a reporter, and later an editorial writer, for the *Minneapolis Tribune*, and you wrote about many events that you might otherwise have initiated as a native advocate. How did you get into newspaper work?

GV: Mostly by chance, resistance, and a smart, accusative lecture in the late sixties at a conference of newspaper editors at the University of Minnesota. I was invited to lecture on native issues and tried my best to shame the editors for publishing *indian* stereotypes in their newspapers. I marched up and down the aisle, trying to make my points more personal and direct. They applauded my performance, of course, and then Bower Hawthorne, the executive editor of the *Minneapolis Tribune*, tracked me down outside the auditorium and handed me his card. His praise was understated, his gesture an unintended insult, and his manner more strategic than curious. He wanted me to come by his office for a conversation. At the time, in the presence of other radical lecturers, his invitation was an obvious maneuver, or so it seemed at the time, but the actual reason was not obvious. I threw his card away and forgot about the episode.

ARL: Wonderful insult, but it also led to a serious job as a reporter?

GV: He sent a reporter to find me, to explain that he was serious about the invitation. So we met, and he offered me a position as an editorial columnist. He wanted me to write about the issues raised in my lecture. The title sounded great, but the idea of editorial writing seemed too passive at the time. I was on the street, on the line as a native advocate, and working at the same time on the case of Thomas White Hawk, who had been sentenced to death for murder in South Dakota. Hawthorne was good about his invitation, and he got my response several months later, after the publication of my investigative report on White Hawk in the *Twin Citian Magazine*. I had traveled for about six months and spent my life savings on the investigation, writing, and organizing a movement against capital punishment in South Dakota. I was broke, flat broke, and worried not only about the rent due but my debts.

ARL: What drew you to the case of Thomas White Hawk?

GV: Maybe he was the eternal native other, the demon at the heart of mother hurt, blood rage, and erotic separation. I don't know the reasons, but he continues to be part of my life. I had rented an office in downtown Minneapolis to work on a novel and, as usual, took my coffee to read the morning newspaper. That was the beginning, a wire service story that White Hawk had been sentenced to capital punishment. I could not go on with my other work that morning. I read the story over and over and then outlined my thoughts about what had happened to this bright, handsome, native student. My thoughts were concise, not much more than a few words and phrases. I wrote that he had been beaten, separated from his family, sexually abused, encouraged to be a proud *indian*, a simulation, and that he suffered from cultural schizophrenia. He might have become a medical doctor, or a man of many tragic poses, a lover, a military man, an athlete, but instead he landed on death row at the South Dakota State Penitentiary.

I studied the crime, interviewed relatives, teachers, and others, examined the court transcripts, and then published an investigative report on the case. Several thousand copies of the report were circulated around the world. That free publication was the reason so many people contributed money to save White Hawk from the electric chair. White Hawk, however, was not very interested in saving his own life at first. He needed a lawyer he could trust, a man who could give him a reason to live. Douglas Hall, a labor lawyer who had worked with us on protests over the years, agreed to visit White Hawk. They talked several times over two days, and that was the start of a legal defense. White Hawk bonded with his lawyer, as he might with an uncle, and became active in his own case.

That evening we stopped for dinner at a restaurant on our way back to Minneapolis. We were both relieved and confident that we could move ahead with the legal remedies to reverse the death sentence. I was about to present a check to Douglas Hall for ten thousand dollars as the first contribution to the legal defense fund, when he surprised me with a formal demand that he could not continue working on the case unless he received much more than that in advance. The generous activist, and civil rights lawyer, had deceived me over dinner with a fee schedule. I should have been more ironic at the time. I should have suggested that he take the case on contingency, and he would be paid if his client lives. My check was part of the unsolicited money that my friend Ronald Libertus had received from readers of my report on the case. Hall made his demand for money only hours after he became the attorney of record for White Hawk. That bond could not be broken over the crease of money. I sat in silence.

Hall never knew that he was about to receive a check. I did not speak to him for several weeks, but our trust was stronger than money manners and we continued to work together. Libertus turned over the check and other money accounts to the Episcopal Church in South Dakota.

White Hawk's capital punishment conviction was commuted by the governor. The commutation was not because of any legal arguments or maneuvers, but because my report brought so much negative attention to the state. The number of summer tourists and autumn game hunters had declined that year. The governor, it seemed, considered the state economy and decided to save White Hawk.

ARL: What has become of White Hawk?

GV: White Hawk was never paroled, but that petition was made several times. I visited him a few years ago, and he did not seem to be in good health. He was active in native spiritual ceremonies, and that gave him a sense of meaning. He died last year of an apparent heart attack in his cell at the South Dakota State Penitentiary.

ARL: Will you write more about the case now?

GV: Maybe a narrative based on his visions of captivity.

ARL: Next, you made the move to journalism?

GV: Yes, my investigative report, *Thomas James White Hawk*, appeared in the *Twin Citian Magazine* at the same time it was published as a pamphlet and distributed around the world. Meanwhile, the trial judge, James Bandy, who had sentenced White Hawk to death without a trial, issued a contempt citation against me for statements attributed to him in my report. Judge Bandy told me that he was opposed to capital punishment and explained that he was rather removing White Hawk from the world because, in his view, there was not much chance of rehabilitation.

That citation made me part of the news stories on the case, and that resulted in a separate invitation to meet with the city editor of the *Minneapolis Tribune*. My investigative report, that meeting, and the previous invitation, all came together. So a real job offer was not to be overlooked. Even so, my decision to write for a newspaper was not without some resistance. I insisted on being hired as a general assignment reporter rather than as an editorial columnist. Hawthorne agreed, and that was my start as a journalist. The only thing left to do was figure out how to actually write a news story by the next day. I was given a desk in the newsroom. I remember the teasing, the great play of language, of irony, and the outrageous, hilarious, skeptical turns and poses of other journalists. I loved the energy there, the pitch, the contradictions of that place from the very first day. Frank Premack, the city editor, and writers Joe Rigert, Sam Newlund, Molly Ivins, Catherine Watson, Jonathan Friendly, and many others, of course, are players in my best memories of that time. My nostalgia for journalism must be the wit and pleasure of contradictions, the tease of manners, and the insecurities of tough love, because no other occupation has ever touched me in that way.

ARL: So you began when?

GV: I started on June 3, 1968, and was amused that no one at the *Minneapolis Tribune* had ever asked me if I could type or drive, the two most important skills for a newspaper reporter. I could do both, of course, but pretended otherwise for two days. This, my first tease, the maneuver of a newcomer, must have earned me a toehold on a tricky presence in the newsroom. I wrote in my autobiography, *Interior Landscapes*, that on the first day an assistant city editor told me to write a practice story. I wrote in my own cursive hand and delivered my story with a note to make a carbon copy for me when it was typed. Dick Youngblood, a chain smoker then, steadied his pronouns and told me, "We type our own stories around here."

"That's news to me."

"You can type, right?"

"No, not me."

"With two fingers?"

"No, never was good at typing."

"How the hell did you get here then?"

"Normal course of events."

"Jesus Christ, this is a first."

Youngblood moved closer, in a cloud of cigarette smoke, and leaned over my desk, right over my typewriter. He was absolutely astounded by my simple question, "By the way, how do you get around?" I was tempted to push the pose of innocence and ask if the company provided chauffeurs for reporters, but decided only to smile and wait for an answer. He was breathless.

"You don't drive either?"

"No one asked about typing and driving."

"Premack, what is this shit?"

Frank Premack, the wily city editor, roared from the other side of the newsroom. He was on to me, but said nothing to his assistant. Premack was a natural, wild teaser, an operatic character. He was tender, cursed and praised for his editorial decisions. I admired him very much, and even now, touched by his memory, mourn his sudden death by heart failure. Frank was a great friend who taught me overnight how to be a journalist. He once told me that the Second Coming of Christ is worth a page and a half of copy, and to keep that in mind in my news story.

ARL: This was exactly the time of Robert Kennedy's death?

GV: Senator Robert Kennedy died of gunshot wounds in Los Angeles, California. There was no teasing in the newsroom that day. Sirhan Sirhan was indicted for murder. Premack told me to write a feature news story that we were *not*, in essence, a violent nation. This was the test, the real test of a journalist. Three days as a reporter and my first assignment was a story that would controvert the public notions of violence. My first byline story appeared on the front page of the feature section of the *Minneapolis Tribune* on June 9, 1968. "So, you can type after all," said Youngblood.

ARL: You quickly found yourself writing about native issues, native politics, the American Indian Movement. What kinds of scrapes and arguments did this lead to?

GV: Clyde Bellecourt, one of the many radical heavies in the American Indian Movement, was on my case for several years because of my editorial series in the *Minneapolis Tribune*. Clyde had grown accustomed to the favors of liberal reviews and was not pleased to read my critical comments about his activities a few days before the occupation of Wounded Knee, South Dakota. I was worried at the time, but to be in his crosshairs is no real distinction. He names so many enemies, for one slight of word or another, and has seldom said a kind word about anybody.

Bellecourt, as it turned out, was camped for two weeks with other natives in a downtown motel in Rapid City, South Dakota.

I was in the motel too, but had arrived late that night and had no idea they were there. Someone told me that the radicals were at the Mother Butler Center, a facility owned by the Catholic Church. Clyde was living in comfort at the motel with his followers, and Dennis Banks was camped with his younger disciples in the Catholic Center. Then, early the next morning, Clyde and company were evicted because they had not paid a bill of more than two thousand dollars. "Are these men serious civil rights workers, or are they a bunch of bandits?" asked Donald Barnett, the mayor of Rapid City. "People working for civil rights do not carry guns. I have seen the records of these men, and you can't sit and negotiate with a man who has a gun." No one was arrested at the motel, but the police confiscated many weapons.

"The American Indian Movement could not survive as a revolutionary tribal caravan without the affinity of lawyers and the press and the sympathy of the church," I wrote twenty-five years ago in the *Minneapolis Tribune*. "The militants speak a language of confrontation and urban politics. They were not elected to speak for reservation tribal people, nor were they appointed to represent the feelings and political views of elected tribal officials." This, and several other investigative stories about the death of Wesley Bad Heart Bull at Buffalo Gap, South Dakota, the burning of the historic Custer County Court House, the racist views of the president of the Rapid City Common Council, the brilliant legal strategies of native lawyer Ramon Roubideaux, and a report on the occupation of Wounded Knee, is what seemed to trouble Bellecourt. I was the first, and probably the only, journalist to report that *no* hostages had ever been taken at Wounded Knee.

ARL: Wasn't this contrary to most of the stories that appeared?

GV: Obviously, the media needed a better story than the facts would maintain. The United Press International reporter, for instance, was never there, and yet he was the first to report the hostages story. These, no doubt, were the stories that activated the military.

Clyde Bellecourt is an obscure simulation, a postindian radical poser. He was invented by the media and, ironically, sustained as a radical by private, state, and federal agencies. I wrote in *Manifest Manners* that in April 1986 he was busted for selling narcotics to undercover agents of the Drug Enforcement Administration. Bellecourt served almost two years of a five-year federal prison sentence. Apparently, court convictions as a dope dealer and hard time in prison did not seem to diminish his radical pose among liberal lawyers and church leaders.

Dennis Banks and many others in various radical organizations got their start in prisons. There, it seems, new courses on native cultures and traditions were used as a sort of postindian recovery program. So many good liberals, many of whom had graduated from notable professional schools, took up the cause of radical posers. Could the cause, in part, have been a romantic hobby, or an insider adventure with the other, or the kitschy simulations of the best and the bore? What can explain these eternal missions of dominance? The good liberals would never live their own lives according to the conservative traditions and romantic notions they support in the native other. Neither the liberals nor the radical posers had much more than a media simulation as a constituency. Now an incredible revolution is at hand, and that house of radical simulations is tumbling down around every postindian casino on a reservation. The truth is stranger than fiction, and in this case, casino greed is greater than radical poses and native traditions. Sovereignty and the liberal romance of natives is at stake, and in the end it might be difficult to distinguish the losers from the winners.

ARL: Where does Dane White come in the story?

GV: Banks, Bellecourt, and others were slow to move against capital punishment in South Dakota. In fact, they never were active in the movement to save Thomas White Hawk. At times, these postindian radicals would leap at the headlines to pose their ideologies in the name of native victimry. The American Indian Movement, for instance, accused a county sheriff for the tragic suicide of Dane White. Bellecourt attempted many appropriations, but this one was wrong and only hurt the good people who were troubled that a native boy was detained in jail for no other crime than truancy. The sheriff in this case was the good guy, because it was the boy's *indian* father who insisted that his son be held in jail to teach him lesson. The radicals took their potshots at the wrong parties, but none of this seemed to matter in the course of radical ideologies.

Frank Premack left an urgent message for me in Bemidji, Minnesota. I had been working on a story about economic development on the Red Lake Reservation. I returned late to the motel and was told by the city editor to cover the funeral services for Dane White the next morning in Sisseton, South Dakota. Dane was thirteen years old at the time of his death, and he had been held in jail for more than a month. The sheriff took the boy along with him on his daily runs, and often he and his wife brought the boy to their home for dinner. Anything, the sheriff said, to mitigate the harsh reality of being alone overnight in a jail cell. Dane's crime was truancy, and his father would not endorse a release. The judge was on a hunting trip, and that too delayed a regular review of the case. I drove all night and arrived just in time for the services. Premack's tease that the Second Coming of Christ is worth a page and a half came to mind in the telephone booth later that morning. This is twice a story now, to honor the memory of Dane White. I dictated my story, which appeared on the front page of the *Minneapolis Tribune*, November 21, 1968.

> Sisseton, South Dakota: Catholic funeral services for Dane White were held here in English and in the Dakota language at Saint Catherine's Indian Mission Church. Following the service, attended by seventy-five people, all but six of whom were Dakota Indians, Dane was buried here in Saint Peter's Catholic Cemetery.
>
> Born in Sisseton thirteen years ago, he took his own life Sunday in the Wilkin County Jail, Breckenridge, Minnesota, where he had been held since October 7 awaiting a juvenile court hearing.
>
> The services and burial for the young Dakota Indian were attended by his father, Cyrus White, Browns Valley, Minnesota; his mother, Burdell Armell, Chicago, Illinois; his maternal and paternal grandparents; his older brother, Timothy, fifteen; three younger sisters, Jodi, twelve, Joan, eleven, and Mary, nine, and many of his school friends.
>
> The Reverend William Keohane conducted the service. Two hymns were sung in the Dakota language. "Dane is here, in the background of the banquet table. Lord remember Dane in your Kingdom," said Father Keohane in prayer, pointing to the large painting of the Last Supper behind the altar of the small Indian church.

Six of Dane's school friends carried his gray metal coffin from the church. Fifteen cars formed the procession to the cemetery on the edge of town. Following the service at the grave, the six young Indian pallbearers removed their honoring ribbons and placed them on the coffin. A cold Dakota wind blew across the slope of Saint Peter's Cemetery. The six pallbearers were the last to leave the grave.

ARL: Then came teaching at colleges and universities, which took you over the years to a number of institutions: Lake Forest College, Bemidji State University, University of Minnesota, University of Oklahoma, University of California, Santa Cruz, and to your present position at Berkeley. What drew you to a life inside the university?

GV: Robert, once more, the word *chance* comes to mind. Yes, chance, in a conversation about a movie with a new friend who, at the time, was teaching at Lake Forest College in Illinois. Actually, there were two reasons, both experience and chance. The first was my frustration that so many radical posers were celebrated and protected by so many needy liberals. Once the nation took up the simulations of so many radical postindians as leaders and turned to consumer sundance traditions, it was time for me to return to literature.

The second reason was the pleasure of chance. I met Jerry Gerasimo, who was on the faculty at Lake Forest College, on the street outside a hotel, at a conference on *indian* education in Minneapolis. I was leaving the conference, critical of the content of the lectures, and he was arriving eager to learn about natives. He studied my reactions, and then we talked for several hours about the film *Easy Rider*. At heart, he was a teaser with a clean smile and a renaissance saunter. That, our wordplay, stories, cuts at simulations, and our critique of lives as concepts, and we became good friends almost overnight. I was a journalist at the time and had no real interest in teaching. However, my mind was changed during the actual interview at Lake Forest College. This is hard to believe, but my first teaching job was in the social science department. I was hired because the chair of the department liked my haiku poems. Now, that was my kind of world. So movie double-talk and my books of haiku created the chance to teach in college.

George Mills, the chair of the department at the time, invited me to dinner and the final interview. I watched his great, bushy eyebrows and tried to sound smart and tricky about the social sciences. "Fuck the social sciences," he roared and then beat the end of the table with his hands. The dishes bounced, and that could have been the end of the interview. Not so. He turned to me, a wild light in his eyes, and said I was there because of my haiku. The social sciences were dead, haiku was not. Then he recited a haiku poem. Basho was his favorite.

Haiku was the chance that became my signature, and the connections have been warm, wild, and memorable. Edward Copeland, my professor of Japanese literature, answered my original haiku with one his own, and we became friends. George Mills gave me my first job as a college teacher because of my haiku. He trusted my creation of a good haiku more than the manners of the social sciences. George Raft was the chance of my conception. Japan was my chance at the end of the alphabet, and haiku was a second chance at Lake Forest College.

ARL: About thirty years ago you started working in Indian studies programs, in Minnesota, Oklahoma, and California. What has your experience been in this new area of study?

GV: Native studies programs, the first such academic areas of study in the history of the nation, were started at several universities in the late sixties. I had taken leave from the *Minneapolis Tribune*, taught a year at Lake Forest College, and then returned to direct a teacher training program at the public school district in Park Rapids, Minnesota. Natives were bused from Pine Point on the White Earth Reservation. Only one out of ten natives ever graduated from the high school, and that created an obvious desegregation problem. The program was funded by a federal agency, and my job was to initiate training sessions with teachers and staff that might change the high dropout rate of native students. My first official act was to call a summer meeting of two school boards, the native elementary school on the reservation and the nearby high school. We met in the old federal school, and as usual, the high school board members were seated on time at the conference table. The native board members were late and took their seats against the wall, as far away from the townies as they could get. The scene was ironic, but not surprising, because the board members were not strangers.

Suddenly lightning flashed, and thunder rattled the building, and the wind howled in the huge ventilators. The sky turned greenish, trees were uprooted, and the board members took cover in the basement of the old federal school. There, crowded together, the two boards were closer in a concrete enclosure, once a coal bin, than they had been for many years. As the thunderstorm roared over the school the board members started telling stories about family, famous baseball games between town and reservation teams. This was my father's generation, and the two boards had known each other since childhood. The storm brought out their stories, the tease of their memories, but once the thunder stopped so did the good humor. Back in the conference room the two boards took their usual positions, townies at the table, natives against the walls.

The Park Rapids teachers were dedicated, the administrators were mannered, and everyone seemed to love the *indians* from the reservation. That, at least in one way, was a contradiction. The simulations of *indians* were better understood than the actual *anishinaabe* students bused to the school in town. The teachers were sensitive, but even so nine out of ten natives in the late sixties quit and never returned to high school in Park Rapids.

ARL: Then you began teaching at Bemidji State?

GV: Bemidji State University hired me to direct a native studies program in the early seventies. My experiences there were unlike any other in native studies. Most of the native students were *anishinaabe* from three nearby reservations, White Earth, Red Lake, and Leech Lake. The students were much closer to their families and communities, and that made a significant difference in the academic and cultural activities on the campus. I convinced the administration, by a tricky money maneuver, to turn over a house that was about to be razed for a parking lot. The Oshki Anishinaabe Family Center became a very active native student center on campus.

My first proposal to establish the center was denied by a senior administrator at Bemidji State University. Meanwhile, a rumor came my way that this same administrator had a shoebox full of cash in his closet. Various campus activities, such as the sale of books and curios, raised a significant amount of cash that was not reported at the time to the state. So, with this in mind, my second proposal was embraced, and we were even given a small budget to maintain the native center. I told the good administrator, taking a chance that there might be something to the rumor, that no one would ever mention his cash stash at the Oshki Anishinaabe Family Center.

ARL: What was different at the University of Minnesota?

GV: The Department of American Indian Studies at the University of Minnesota was, at first, one of the best in the country. I had been teaching at the University of California, Berkeley, when Minnesota hired me to teach Native American literature and related courses. I continued to teach at Berkeley during the winter quarters, and then, in a few years, the Department of American Indian Studies was terminated at Minnesota. Once, in the best of times, there were more than a dozen faculty, and two native languages were taught. Unfortunately, the faculty was so rancorous and divided after a decade of service that no one could restore a sense of trust or confidence in the subject. The dean notified the faculty that we had one year to reorganize the department. I could not convince my colleagues that the department might be terminated if we did not act. Nothing happened, and near the end of that academic year the dean reminded the faculty of his decision and advised us to find other academic homes. The dean pulled the plug on the department in the early eighties. My position was moved to American Studies.

The tricky stories were better at the very end, when the movers arrived and carried away the dead miniature birch tree. I published a story in *Earthdivers* that established the Chair of Tears. Captain Shammer, the first trickster to hold the ironic, celebrated chair in the native studies department, was hired because he was the least qualified, and that made perfect sense because, in the past, the best and brightest natives were hired, and each one failed to restore the confidence of the department. So why not try the opposite? Shammer changed the name to Undecided Studies, founded the Halfbreed Hall of Fame, and then offered the department for sale to the highest bidder, lock, stock, and barrel.

Rose Shingobe, the late, mighty backbiter, taught the *anishinaabe* language in the department. This tricky story comes after years of her nasty comments behind my back, and in my face at department meetings. Not at every meeting, but her negative energy was always imminent. She was haunted by the fact that my father's cousin, Joe Vizenor, who was then business manager of the Minnesota Chippewa Tribe, had done something against her family. She was always angry, but never clear about the cause of the trouble. So she would attack me with obscure accusations because of my surname. This went on for years, and some of my friends tried to intervene. They even tried to trick her out of the obsession over my name, but nothing changed the scene.

Then, late one afternoon, in a dark, departmental hallway, a great shamanic bear arose in me. Rose was alone at the other end of the hallway, on her way out of the building. I posed as a bear, my arms, paws, in motion, and roared at her in the hallway. She stopped and waited in silence. I told her in a surly tone of voice that if she ever backbit me again the bear would cause her more trouble than Joe Vizenor. She moved her head but said nothing. The bear turned around in the dark and vanished on the elevator. She ran down eight flights of stairs to the street. Rose never mentioned the bear, and she never again said a bad word about me. She even teased me at times, but very cautiously.

ARL: Surely the end of the department was not a tragic story. Could this be a peculiar turn of victimry? How could there be such a failure?

GV: Robert, the stories were never tragic. More than anything, maybe there was a failure of irony, and that because of *indian* simulations. Some of the teachers at that time seemed to be caught in an *indian* persona that was against academic thought. The faculty wore many masks, which is not unusual, but there wasn't much beneath their masks. Their poses were an absence, not a native presence. The faculty was paranoid, the staff were sullen, and they argued about everything. There were bitter, irreconcilable differences. The faculty lost the native tease and missed the irony, and one of the great native studies department came to an end in silence.

The politics of native communities was certain to influence academic programs. Sometimes the posers and revisionists even tried to change the very courses we taught. The burdens of administration never seemed to end in native studies, and no matter how wise or responsible the leader, there were always doubts about *indian* identity, and destructive rumors were an ordinary part of conversations. I endured the end of native irony at the University of Minnesota.

ARL: Then you and your wife, Laura Hall, a Britisher of Chinese descent, left Minnesota in 1983 to teach at Tianjin University in the People's Republic of China. You were moved to write a novel out of that experience, but how difficult was it to leave a tenured position?

GV: I wanted no more of the backbiters and was pained beyond reason by destructive identity politics. So the farther we could get from native studies the better. I was ready to move out of the country, and as it turned out we both found teaching jobs at Tianjin University in the People's Republic of China.

Tianjin is a huge city, about seven million people. We were given a very comfortable apartment in a guest house for foreign teachers. At the time there were only about fifty foreigners in the city. We were always the focus of public attention. I remember standing at the window of a department store and looking in at a bicycle on display. Suddenly there were hundreds of faces reflected in the glass. I turned and faced a crowd of curious people. Mostly, it seemed to me at the time, they wanted to get a closer look at my big nose. They were polite, and silent, and must have wondered what was so interesting about a bicycle in the window. This was the summer the government allowed street markets to operate in the city, and overnight, as if millions of closet marketeers had stashed their stock, there were vendors selling everything from shirts to caged songbirds, from bread to rat leather shoes.

I was taken with the rituals of a man and his caged chickens. He was strong and certain as he prepared a chicken for sale. Name your chicken in one of the cages, and the man would bind the legs, wings, and neck of the bird with one hand and cut the throat of the chicken with the other. The bird shivered, blinked, as blood ran slowly into a dish. I wrote about this man and his ritual in *Griever: An American Monkey King in China*. I was also inspired by the stone man and wrote about him in my novel.

He was skinny, an old man, but his meditation and rituals over round river stones were shamanic. He teased the crowd, paced around the stones on the back of a bicycle cart, and then he struck the stone with the side of his hand, breaking clean wide slivers from the memory of the stone. I could have easily followed that shaman into the country, far, far from native studies, at the drop of a stone. *Griever* was my meditation with that great stone man.

ARL: And your wife, Laura?

GV: Laura taught English to graduate students who were aspiring to graduate business programs in the United States and Canada. And I taught English and American literature to advanced undergraduates. They were formal, always polite, and eager to learn about popular culture, pronunciation, and colloquialisms. I was touched by their selection, the chance of their education. They were the choice of masters who carried out the Cultural Revolution. Their education was politically determined, understated, and evasive.

Laura's students once asked her, in an unguarded moment, if she could explain the meaning of Buddhism. The shocking contradiction is that the common knowledge of a repressed religion must be delivered by outsiders. At the time, even the question was a political risk. I worried about my ironic presence there, at the very absence of a great culture, and carried on in awkward and hesitant conversations the obvious similarities of *indian* simulations and the absence of cultural memory. Yes, most of my students had heard about the *red indians*, but their interests were in material conversions, not in the ironies of tricksters.

Then, once more by chance, the *anishinaabe* trickster created an ironic presence, this time in an operatic production of *Havoc of Heaven*, about the Chinese Monkey King. This great mind monkey is related to the mighty trickster of my stories. They were both conceived in stone and create fantastic stories of liberation and survivance. These tricksters ducked the censure of missionaries, anthropologists, and the commie revisionists. The Monkey King was never converted to overthrow wicked landlords or serve the literal ideologies of the Cultural Revolution. Either the commies and anthropologists could not understand irony, or else they were worried about comic retribution.

The Chinese Monkey King and Naanabozho, the *anishinaabe* trickster, never court the deadbeat stories of victimry. These characters can trick a wise man right out of his library card, adjectives, underwear, and fate. I brought these two tricky literary figures together in my novel *Griever: An American Monkey King in China*. Griever de Hocus comes to teach literature at Zhou Enlai University in Tianjin. Griever carried out every one of my tricky fantasies of survivance, political conversions, and subversions of the corrupt, deadhead commies at the university.

2

Autobiographies

ARL: Let's talk about your autobiography, *Interior Landscapes*. Many people see a contradiction in the idea of "Indian autobiography," the conflict of oral and scriptural traditions. Did that bother you, the writing of a native life story?

GV: No, not really. Listen, oral stories are natural, and to the ear, a distinctive sense of the visionary, and written words are to the eye, or at least to an inner voice of memories. One is sound, the other a crucial silence. Native stories are sound and vision, and both are survivance. My presence is in written stories, and we must come together in the book or be lost to manners and discoveries.

I was sure that someone would read the stories of my life, a literary life, because people have listened to my stories. I create my life in oral stories, and so create my life in the book. Chances, not causes, are my stories. I tried in my autobiography to relate the chance and ironies of my experiences. Chance is my best sense of the *real*, and chance must deny the cause of victimry. I was also convinced that there were eager readers for any original native literary autobiography. I was not sure, however, that readers would be interested in a crossblood autobiography. No surprise to me that many readers go for the categories that are written, more or less, to satisfy their common expectations. The native sense of chance, the very chance of conception as a human and a crossblood, and my constant tease of postindian identities touch many readers, but not those who search for authentic *indian* simulations.

I approached the writing of an autobiography with some resistance. Not the myths and metaphors of *Interior Landscapes*, but my very first autobiographical essay, which was published in *Growing Up in Minnesota*, edited by Chester Anderson. I mean to say that he had invited me to contribute an autobiographical essay to his book, a collection of essays by Minnesota writers.

I declined, at first, because I could not imagine writing about myself as a character. I was not an isolated self and could not think about myself without the presence of many others. Chet Anderson refused to accept my decision. He knew better, and he was right.

James Olny, at about that time, edited a collection of critical essays about autobiography. Most of my questions were answered by the essays, or at least my concern and resistance had a critical context that other writers had thought carefully about. I remember Georges Gusdorf wrote that for most of human history people did not oppose others to create an individual self. So my autobiography had to be written in a different style. I argued that there was a voice, and a pose of a self, but no literary form in autobiography. I overcame my resistance to this idea of absence and created my own style. I created myself as one of many characters, in many situations, and gave voices to others who might have something to say about me. Later, *Interior Landscapes: Autobiographical Myths and Metaphors* was written in that style.

ARL: Well, you say there is no form, but in fact, there are twenty-nine sequences, each one implying at least a parallel or a mutuality with the other. Perhaps, if you like, a hall of mirrors in the reading of the sequences. That is a form, in a certain kind of way?

GV: My stories in *Interior Landscapes* are episodes of memory, in a style that creates the presence of others, as the situational form of *me*, a me as a literary self of chance. I consider this style to be an ordinary source of recollections, that is, an episodic, social, visionary form of consciousness, and a tease of self-creation. In other words, I remember certain episodes and write stories about them. The episodes, or descriptive events, that are associated in some way with strong emotions are enhanced by the presence of others in stories.

ARL: In two other major contemporary native autobiographies, *The Names* by Scott Momaday and *Storyteller* by Leslie Silko, the issue of voice, of ventriloquy, is very much to the forefront of things. You speak of "my crossblood remembrance." Is that a fair indication of the form as well as the substance of *Interior Landscapes*?

GV: Yes, my autobiographical stories and episodes are a crossblood remembrance. I try to avoid the first person pronoun, but that, of course, is not always possible in the construction of scenes from memory. I refer to myself as a character and do so in the presence of others in the story, as my sources of memory are not separations. So to construct myself only as a first person, in that mighty, ultimate pronoun of exclusive identity, is to misplace that sense of presence and survivance. The pronoun, as an interior voice, is converted anew by the reader.

ARL: Trickster pronouns?

GV: Yes, the trickster Naanabozho as an elusive pronoun.

ARL: Is it part of your own trickster practice to be at once first person singular and plural, first and third person?

GV: The pleasures of Naanabozho, the trickster, is complicated not in oral stories but in *indian* simulations. There is chance, tricky irony, and wild language play in both oral and written stories. The trouble is in the literal curse of language, the will to determine and represent the person, the mode, manner, and motivation of the voice, and to maintain the other in a pronoun over conversions and ironies. I am not the pronoun, but the ironic presence of a native noun. I rush at times to a tricky style, an original literary practice in writing trickster stories. The word itself, *tricky, trickster*, is resisted by many readers as a representation of cunning deception rather than chance and liberation in stories. The trickster suggests bad manners, at least, and deception of a kind that is not culturally acceptable in the best of families. Fairly, some readers might argue, as the word carries on in a world of thieves. The trickster is a tease in stories, not in real life. Tricksters are better than the real, much better than flesh and blood, because Naanabozho and other tricksters are stories of liberation, not mere representations. Tricky transformation, not the separation of the other, and not savagism. The trickster is a very sophisticated literary practice in *anishinaabe* stories.

ARL: You start with creation and trickster stories, and yet preface your stories with contemporary literary names, such as Eudora Welty, Primo Levi, Michel Foucault, and Jean Baudrillard. That's a long jump from native tricksters, or is it?

GV: Maybe a jump, but it is synchronous in the sense that trickster stories, oral or written, and contemporary theories are not developmental ideas. I mean, the pleasures of tricky language have always been with us and could be more established than manners, in the ironic sense that the earliest uses of language might have been more tricky and deceptive than representational. George Steiner makes this point, that the first need to utter a word was to deceive someone. Why else would one be so driven to speak if things were so clearly represented?

Maybe language has always been deceptive, if for no other reason, to avoid boredom and the mundane. Trickster stories, then, might be the aesthetic pleasure of deception and liberation. Trickery and ironic stories are advantages. My point is that this is such a common experience that storiers have always been about the practice. My sense of stories is enriched by many associations with this practice. Please, set aside the word *tradition*, as in "*indian* traditions," because it suggests that trickster stories, irony, and the originary deception of language, is a cultural and determined practice. That, a trickster tradition, would be an ironic tease and a natural contradiction. Tradition, as you know, is a tamer, not a liberator. Now, to court the trickster out of sound and into the book, and the silence of the page, is a deception of another sort. Tricky courage comes from those writers and post-modern theorists who have thought about these matters, and who have created a theoretical language of discourse, aesthetic deception, deconstruction, and survivance.

ARL: So it makes perfect sense to bring that oral communal body of reference into a relation with some of the modern names of contemporary cultural theory?

GV: Quite so, and the demands upon a better language of interpretation, you know, in current thought, are probably similar demands that were once brought to oral stories. Native storiers had to create better stories, trickster stories of survivance. My stories stand for survivance, and yet there is nothing more significant than the ordinary play of language. So the critique of language and literature today is something similar to what native storiers must have done, as they were overburdened with authority, healer dealers, and the politics of tradition in stories. Trickster stories break out of the heavy burdens of tradition with a tease of action and a sense of chance. That, then, is the threshold of native survivance.

ARL: You pursue in your autobiography, *Interior Landscapes*, these mutually enfolded worlds of native, white, crossblood, city, reservation, of America and Japan, Japan to America. Is the voice you are aiming for one that can move across every domain?

GV: I am a storier, and my stories enfold the creation of a voice, a time, and a place that is always in motion, or visionary transmotion. And the stories create me. I say that because the circumstances of reading and critical interpretation create stories and the storier. I tease these ideas in my stories and create a voice and sense of presence.

ARL: How, then, do you respond to Arnold Krupat's notion of synecdoche in native autobiography? Does synecdoche hold in your stories?

GV: Arnold Krupat was one of the first interpreters of native life stories and autobiography, and he observed a distinctive literary practice that was different from what he found in other autobiographies. He brought our attention to the fact that native autobiographers, for the most part, begin their life stories with some reference to a larger community or tribal association, and then relate the individual to the family and community. The point he makes, theoretically, is wise and very perceptive: that in contrast to other autobiographies, natives start with a larger picture and then relate that to the self. The notion of synecdoche, then, is that the self comes out a history, or that native identity is first part of a community. There are very few references, if any, to a larger community at the start of other autobiographical stories. The exceptions, of course, would be those religious or nationalistic autobiographies.

My autobiographical stories were published long before Krupat's theory. So I was surprised to learn that my autobiographical stories were synecdochic, in the sense that my life story started with an *anishinaabe* family history. This creates, of course, a context of authority and native presence. The contradiction is that the individual storier creates a history and an image, or persona, but the storier does not create an absolute self.

The autobiography does not speak for the community, and stories do not represent the self. The synecdochic persona is a pose, and a trope of the moment. Maybe, in some senses, a communal trope is more than a pose, but pronouns are the tease of synecdochic nouns.

My sense of presence in a name, or a pronoun, is not unitary, objective, or a separation. Krupat, in his critique of autobiographies, seems to have overlooked the obvious, that natives are not as communal as he might want them to be in theory. What I mean to say is that natives are probably the most individualistic people of any communities in the world. Consider the value of individual visions, the value of individual descriptive dreams and nicknames. In other words, the many ceremonies, shamanic visions, practices, and experiences in native communities are so highly individualistic, diverse, and unique, that romantic reductions of tradition and community as common sources of native identity are difficult to support, even in theory.

Native visions are an originary sense of presence, and the stories of such unique individual experiences are a contradiction of the communal notions of synecdoche. Consider the visions of a healer, the dangerous meditation and travels of shamans. The vision of the shaman is not like any other vision in the world. The sources of visions and identity, and the creation of the self, are more individualistic than communal. These visions and stories are more than communal, and must tease traditions. No one else has ever had such a vision. The vision is a separation and disassociation from ordinary time and space, and from traditions. And the recognition of native visions and nicknames must be earned in communities. That, the recognition of a native presence, is a continuous tease in stories. What is mistaken to be tradition is a visionary sovereignty. Native stories are never the foretaste of synecdoche. Krupat might have posed a synecdochic *indian* irony.

ARL: What of the links of shamanism and autobiography?

GV: Much of creative literature is shamanic because it is a visionary journey, creating a time and a place that did not exist before, and the story creates a sense of presence. Many autobiographical stories are also healing and create a sense of liberation. But again, creative literature of this kind, stories that have a sense of shamanic visions, are dangerous. The shaman returns with a vision and must earn the trust of a community. Similarly, the creative writer must earn a presence in literature and the politics of the time. Shamans earn respect as healers, and so writers must earn their readers, but not as mere consumers. Not every shaman or creative storier works that way, but most literature is handed on by readers and finds some political acceptance among peers. Now, the visionary literature that transforms what we once thought of as a native presence becomes a literature that heals, and a literature that liberates.

ARL: Do you see a move in the direction that you have just described, a shamanic, visionary literature, in the coming generation of writers like Louis Owens, Gordon Henry, and Thomas King?

GV: Louis Owens is a great, visionary author. He creates stories that rise with the rivers, turn with the seasons, and heal readers at the literary littoral. Gordon Henry writes with a generous touch of meditation, an imagistic manner of native dream songs. Thomas King teases anew the manners of tradition, and in his ironic turns and shimmers of the obvious, he does liberate the reader, and the humor in his stories has a healing power.

ARL: What are the visions in your stories?

GV: My first novel, *Bearheart: The Heirship Chronicles*, scared me to creation, to a visionary separation. Late at night, on my walks after writing most of the day, scenes of the novel came alive at every turn, and some of the characters, the most evil, lurked in the alleys, at the darkest intersections. I walked faster and hummed over the menace. I even tried to overcome my fear of the novel by lurking, by pausing in alleys, by courting the unknown to beat the temptations of victimry. The heat of *Bearheart* lasts in my memories; even now the mere mention runs warm in my head and hands.

My novel *Griever* is comic, liberative, and visionary. Most of the scenes are based on historic events and related to my experiences as a teacher in the People's Republic of China. *Dead Voices*, on the other hand, was written in two very distinct visionary states. The first was a shamanic separation from a sense of ordinary reality, a fury of words that were unreadable the next day. I was living alone in Berkeley and teaching native literature at the University of California. The second vision was the actual creation of the stories. *Dead Voices* was created in the heat of four weeks one summer in Norman, Oklahoma. *Hotline Healers* is visionary, in the sense of trickster chance, transformation, and liberation. My novels and some of my stories are shamanic and visionary. Creation must be intense, and so with stories. Sometimes the heat of my writing is a vision of survivance.

3

Haiku Scenes

ARL: Gerald, may we turn to your first publications of original haiku poems? Why did you start your career as a writer with haiku poetry?

GV: I must say, once more, my start as a writer was by chance and the ease of imagistic poetry. Haiku, in a sense, caught me out on the road to nature, and that was my best turn to literature. The tease of nature is in my blood, and that must make visions out of taste and sound, and the outcome, no doubt, is more imagistic than discovery. Nature is tricky, a constant tease, and even the most obvious native traces of the seasons are creative sensations, a chance of stories. Sometimes that mighty tease of nature comes out in blank verse, but never in my poetry. Now, haiku is my aesthetic survivance.

ARL: Why so?

GV: Listen, my sense of haiku is an imagistic gaze. Yes, a natural gaze, the meditative gaze of visual memories. The turn of nature is in me, and in everyone. So my start was mythic, a tricky sense of motion on the road that connected me to nature, a native presence, and at the same time, my creation is in the book. My haiku poems, and the chance of survivance, created me in nature and the book.

Chance, however, does not reveal the romance of my presence, and certainly not the common risks and doubts of being a writer of imagistic poetry. I was moved to write, to be known in the book, but my brush with literature in public school was not very creative or productive. Most of my literature teachers might have been right, at the time, to rush every sentence with a canon measure. I might not have become a writer if they had done otherwise. Pedagogy was an ironic enforcer, but my sense of visual memories survived the courses, and that was more than enough for me to learn the virtues of resistance. How else could the teachers be sure that only visual memories might survive the manners of a high school education? Maybe my teachers were at their best to scare me out of literature, because their very lessons cut me out of the mannered culture of sonnets.

My visual memories are survivance stories, and the ease of haiku images, even in translation, made immediate sense to me, and that without a canon course in literature. The scenes that carried me were in nature, images of a pond, sunrise on the wings of a dragonfly, the march of a blue heron, cracks in the river ice, the sounds of spring, and not in the obscure cuts of literary histories. The images of haiku are accessible in nature and culture, and that alone was more than any poetry had ever given me in the past. I was amused, at first, by the common, natural scenes in haiku poetry. The imagistic scenes were my nature, and then, later, my thoughts turned to the notion of possession and impermanence, the very tease of my aesthetic presence in nature. Issa comes to mind in the traces of memories and seasons. He remembers, in *The Year of My Life*, the death of his daughter in this haiku translated by Nobuyuki Yuasa:

> the world of dew
> is the world of dew
> and yet . . .
> and yet . . .

I was eighteen years old at the time, and every haiku moment was a scene of my presence and survivance. Haiku was a great gift, and yet the images were my first memorable flights of impermanence. The United States Army, by chance, sent me to serve in northern Japan. There haiku caught me on the road as a soldier and turned me back to the seasons, back to the memories of my own nature. The turns and conversions of haiku were not exotic, because nature is my sense of presence, not discovery. My haiku scenes are similar, in a sense, to the images in *anishinaabe* dream songs, and now these mythic connections seem so natural to me. Once, worlds apart in time and place, these images came together by chance. Many *anishinaabe* dream songs are about the presence of animals in visions. My haiku are the same, and yet, and yet, the contradiction that imagistic scenes are my impermanence and survivance. Haiku poems were my very first creations, and since then imagistic scenes of nature are always present in my writing. The presence of nature in my novels, even in my essays, is an imagistic survivance as an author. My survivance is in nature and the book.

ARL: As if you understood your own call to be a writer?

GV: More than a call, that first tease of haiku was my conversion, and maybe a visionary transformation, at least in my aesthetic survivance in nature. Yet these imagistic moments, the very scenes of my creation in literature, are elusive, a natural turn with the seasons, or, "a stone, a leaf, a door," in the words of the novelist Thomas Wolfe.

ARL: Gerald, was it your ambition to "Americanize" haiku? In your most recent haiku, for instance, you create envois with each poem, an original style. I don't mean just the form, but the subjects you pick, the native memories, and the use of nature in Minnesota?

GV: Not mere ambition, but creation, and my haiku scenes are the tease of seasons, not cultures or nations. The seasons create the haiku scenes, and the images are common, not exotic. What comes to mind, of course, are my memories of seasons on the run in Minnesota. One morning, the traces of winter in the autumn, and later, the rush of spring on the twig, in the sumac near the river, and my conversions, season after season, in the curve of the sun and wild shadows at the treelines. My haiku come out of these experiences and memories, and my very creation, in a sense, is that pause to create the seasons, the very visions of me in nature. I am a ghost writer of nature, and the conversions, the mythic turns of the solstice, tease the sumac and sparrows, catkins and cedar waxwings, thunder and bears, and yet, and yet, here we are in the book. I wonder if my presence is created in the haiku scenes of the seasons. Sometimes, the pauses in nature are memories, the scenes of my presence. The seasons are sounds, the thunder of ice cracking on the lake, and the creases of the wind on a spiderweb. My creation is that pause in nature, and haiku scenes are the rights of my impermanence in the book. And my sense of presence, then and now, is in the images of great haiku poets.

Yosa Buson, the son of a farmer, was born more than two centuries ago, and his haiku scenes come to me as a presence in translation, and so we meet by nature in the book. He was a cultural dilettante and, at the same time, a brilliant haiku poet. Buson wrote about the seasons and teased his own transience. He was not devoted to nature, as other poets were, but he created exquisite imagistic poems. R. H. Blyth, in *Haiku: Eastern Culture*, translates this haiku by Buson:

> winter rain
> a mouse runs
> over the koto

I wrote back to him one winter with this haiku poem:

> cold rain
> field mice rattle the dishes
> buson's koto

The koto, as you know, is a stringed instrument. Buson's transience, the nature of haiku, and my flights of impermanence came together with others in the tricky imagistic seasons of the book.

ARL: One of the things that strikes me in your haiku is the humor – the humor and trickster resonance that come of the tension between insects and culture, or as you write in this haiku, between flies, natural rhythm, and pink grapefruit, as follows:

> fat green flies
> square dance on the pink grapefruit
> honor your partners

GV: Matsuo Basho might have created that last line, *honor your partners*. Nature is honored by his haiku and *haibun* meditation, and his subtle humor on the road. He was a generous wanderer who turned to Zen Buddhism and devoted most of his experiences and memories to the imagistic truth of nature. Basho might not have posed a square dance of trickster flies, but he was amused on the very day of his death that the flies were delighted and gathered on the sliding screens. Makoto Ueda, in *Basho and His Interpreters*, translated this haiku scene:

> in the seasonal rain
> a crane's legs
> have become short

Kobayashi Issa, however, might have teased the green flies to dance with him right out of the restaurant. His sympathies were always with animals and insects. Issa has a subtle sense of irony. One of my favorite haiku poems was published in *World within Walls* by Donald Keene:

skinny frog
don't be discouraged
issa is here

Robert, my haiku teases the obvious perversion of "human nature," the common will to kill insects, and that is the very tension of the square dance scene on the pink grapefruit. The unstated is not surreal, as flies might dance for their breakfast, but rather a conversion of distaste and dominance. The last line of my haiku, *honor your partners*, must tease the memories of a rural square dance, you know, the allemande turns of couples in the dance. Choose your sides and allemande in a tricky haiku with the fat green flies. That dance of the flies is my aesthetic survivance, and a tease of monotheism, but what is not a tease?

ARL: That's a nice tease, as it is, again, in "White Earth, Images and Agonies." You have a fine line in that poem, "tricksters roam the rearview mirrors." Do most of your poems operate as "rearview mirrors"?

GV: Maybe, and the *animals at the treelines* at the end of that poem *send back the hats and rusted traps*. That direction is a reversion of the beaver in the fur trade, an imagistic ghost dance and return of nature. The images in the mirror come in so many stories, and mine are part of that common play of representations. My imagistic gaze is twice reversed in the rearview mirror. Once as a trickster pose, a transmutation of my presence, and twice, yes twice, as the storier. So you might ask, Who are these teasers, shadows aback, the tricksters that roam at our rear in the wake of the mirror?

ARL: How did poetry help in your development as a writer?

GV: Poetry, and especially haiku, taught me how to hold an imagistic gaze, and that gaze is my survivance. Many chapters in my novels begin with a natural metaphor and create a sense of the season, the tease of a haiku scene. I learned how to create tension in concise images, by the mere presence of nature. Plum petals in a thunderstorm, bears at the treeline, squirrels at the window, green flies on the grapefruit are a few examples. When my son Robert was in elementary school I visited his classes once or twice a year to talk about haiku poetry. Haiku was accessible, and the students did not have to know much about stories to understand the play of nature and the beast in language. These students were at home with imagistic tension in language. They carried the memories of pets across the street in heavy traffic, hunted mosquitoes in a tent, and teased their teachers.

I said, "Here is one word, and the image of a word, and you give me another word that creates some tension between the words." I said "dog," and they said "traffic," and the tension of a cat was the presence of a dog. These words and images were more than structural associations, because the students actually created the tension by words and the suggestion of motion in visual memory. Regrettably, some teachers have tortured the very best haiku scenes with possessive pronouns and delegated imagistic poetry to a mere lesson in the punctuated evolution of literature.

4

Scripts and Plays

ARL: You bowed in with *Two Wings the Butterfly* in 1962, a pamphlet of haiku poems printed by inmates at the Minnesota State Reformatory in Saint Cloud, and two years later *Raising the Moon Vines*, your first book of haiku, was published in Minneapolis. But you've also long been interested in other literary forms. I want to ask you about your film scenario *Harold of Orange* and your play *Ishi and the Wood Ducks*. What lay behind Harold, the trickster character in your film?

GV: Two things: the actual play of language in the script and the tease of images in *Harold of Orange*. The first, of course, is the dialogue of the characters, and the second thing is the ironic tease of obvious visual images in the film, such as the structural reversal of team names at a baseball game. The natives arrive with the word "anglo" printed on their red T-shirts, and the foundation directors wear the name "indian" on their white T-shirts. Other active scenes of tricky tension are obvious, such as the conversations on the school bus, natives in neckties, human skeletons in a glass case, the play of socioacupuncture, and more.

The script creates an ironic tension too, as the characters announce their tricky schemes and conduct a sacred naming ceremony out of a cigar box in a parking lot. Here, names such as Baltic and Connecticut are the property cards in the game of Monopoly. Harold Sinseer and the other native characters are always at the tease and turn of irony. For instance, as the Warriors of Orange and the directors of the Bily Foundation are riding around on a school bus in the city, Ted Velt, a conservative foundation man, asks Son Bear, "How many Indians were there at the time Christopher Columbus discovered the New World?" Well, first of all, who would know? Even a shaman with a thick memory would turn this unanswerable question around to a tricky fact. Here, the underlying irony is that the foundation man knows everything about the absence of *indians*, an arrogance posed in the questions, and nothing about the presence of natives. He knows too much about the inventions, and movie simulations, but too little about native humor and tricky stories. Son Bear, who wears a Sun Dance Film Festival hat, pauses, removes his earphones, and says, "None, not one." Naturally, this evasion troubles the foundation man. "What do you mean, none?" Son Bear strains to explain that "Columbus never discovered anything, and when he never did he invented Indians because we never heard the word before he dropped by by accident." Velt persists. "Well, let me phrase the question in a different way then. How many tribal people were there here then, ahh, before Columbus invented Indians?" Son Bear pauses once more and then announces, with great authority, "Forty-nine million, seven hundred twenty-three thousand, one hundred and ninety-six on this continent, including what is now Mexico."

I should mention another ironic scene in *Harold of Orange*. The tension, again, is in the word games on the school bus, or the red pinch on the yellow bus of new foundation fools. Andrew Burch asks a Warrior of Orange, "I have considered the origin theories of the American Indians. Some are quite interesting. I find the Bering Strait migration theory to be the most credible. How about you then, what are your thoughts on the subject?" So, here is another question about absence over presence, and the pose is cultural arrogance. New Crows, however, will not be cornered as he plays to the arrogance of the foundation man, "From here to there, we emerged from the flood here, the first people, unless you think we are related to the panda bear." Andrew touches his necktie as he responds, "Actually, what you say makes a great deal of sense, but the problem I seem to have, you see, is that there is so little evidence to support your idea." New Crows smiles and says, "Jesus Christ was an American Indian." Andrew, outwitted in the play of his own arrogance, turns away and says, "Was he now, who would have guessed?" For me the ironies were doubled in the production of the film, as the native actors made the scenes with no acting experience. The others, however, were very practiced and experienced stage and screen actors.

ARL: Would that also hold for your play *Ishi and the Wood Ducks*? The double ironies?

GV: Yes, and there are several structural reversals in my play. Ishi is the subject, the object, the absence, the presence, and the main character in his stories. The play opens on a bench outside a federal court and ends in the First District Court of Character. Ishi is on trial for alleged violations of the Indian Arts and Crafts Act. He is an artist in the play, but could not in fact prove that he was indeed a native. He was, after all, named the last of his tribe, the last stone age man, so how could he prove he was anyone by law?

Justice Alfred Kroeber rules at the end of the play that "Ishi is real and the law is not." He is his own tribe. "Ishi is an artist, he is our remembrance of justice, and that is his natural character." Ishi is present and an active character in the prologue, and the first and last acts. The audience is aware of his ironic presence in the second and third acts, but only his name and ashes in an urn are mentioned by the other characters in the play.

I think these elaborations of absence and presence are more intricate and precise than a mirror image, and more ironic than the mere abstract reversal of consciousness, character, and history. Ishi is a visionary presence, and at the same time, he is an ethnographic absence. He is my tease of a native holoconsciousness, yes, the entire consciousness of natives in the play, and in another sense, my creation is his survivance.

Ishi has a presence in the generous bait and tease of his wood duck stories. He is a voice of memories, and he is wise, witty, and tricky. Ironically, the other characters are the real absence, as they forever hold to their ethnographic discoveries and documents. Ishi is about in every act in the play and hears everything the experts say in his name. He, on the other hand, sits on a bench outside a courtroom and talks with an old woman about names.

> Ishi is my museum name, not my real name.
> Same with me, says Boots.
> Do you have a sacred name?
> Boots, the boys teased me about my boots.
> Ishi is my nickname.
> Boots is my sacred name.
> No one has ever heard my sacred name.
> No one has every heard my real name.

Alfred Kroeber gave me a museum name.
My husband lied to me about our name.

Alfred Kroeber, as you know, was the generous anthropologist who cared for Ishi in a museum at the University of California. Kroeber said he had "perceptive power far keener than those of highly educated white men. He reasons well, grasps an idea quickly, has a keen sense of humor, is gentle, thoughtful, and courteous, and has a higher type of mentality than most Indians." Ishi, it would seem, was the great scout of native discoveries, and should have been given an honorary doctorate. Surely, he was aware of the ironies in his name, because his wood duck stories never ended. Ishi, the tricky museum native, earned his nickname from an anthropologist and he sent one back at the same time. Ishi named Kroeber the "Big Chiep." There, in a name, in his tricky presence, is an ironic reversion of his native absence.

ARL: Gerald, may we turn to another irony, that you were sued by a sculptor in the name of Ishi? Whatever became of that play in court?

GV: That was a year of double ironies, as the trial, my legal play in court, folded over a stage reading of *Ishi and the Wood Ducks* in Chicago. Ishi is both a presence and a silent witness in my play, but only his name was evidence in the actual court trial. Surely, the native tease is eternal in his name, that is, in the ironic scripture of his museum name by anthropology. My play *Ishi and the Wood Ducks* was published in the college anthology *Native American Literature* before Harkin Lucero, the sculptor, sued me over what seemed to be nothing more than the expectations of a retro simulation. Actually, the expectations that became a civil action started a decade earlier, in the late eighties, at the University of California, Berkeley. I had formally proposed that half of Dwinelle Hall be named Ishi Hall. The campus newspaper and student organizations supported the proposal, and many faculty reviewed my idea favorably, if not amused by my naïveté about academic manifest manners. The procedures, as you might expect, were very complicated, but who would have thought at the time that a mere subcommittee, organized at the lowest level of faculty governance, would vote against my proposal to honor the very first native employee of the University of California.

Alfred Kroeber, you remember, had read in the newspaper about this silent native man and arranged, in the late summer of 1911, for him to live and work in the Museum of Anthropology. The museum was then located in San Francisco. Ishi was probably about fifty years old at the time of his fateful discovery by anthropologists. He died of tuberculosis five years later, on March 25, 1916. Yes, and his ashes are now in a small black pot in a niche at Mount Olivet Cemetery, which is near San Francisco. That's where the play and the actual court suit come together. The jury was very interested in what was actually said over the niche, and that is also a scene in my play.

I tried several times to keep my proposal alive on campus, and after eight years another committee offered me a compromise, the first serious consideration, to name a courtyard in his honor. I was very pleased and, as they say, the rest is history, including the jury trail and my play. Ishi Court was dedicated as part of Dwinelle Hall in May 1993. Justice Gary Strankman delivered a very moving commemoration of Ishi, and later, at the reception, several people suggested that we consider a sculpture in Ishi Court.

ARL: Were you considering monuments at the time?

GV: No, that was only a courtesy thought. I was more interested in names and endowments than sculpture, in part, because monuments take too much time and money. But it was a fine dedication and reception and many ideas were brushed with pleasure. Caitlin Croughan was at the commemoration and invited me to meet Harkin Lucero, a local sculptor, and that was the critical start of the retro simulations of Ishi. So we met a few weeks later. Lucero's ambition, it seemed to me at the time, far exceeded his talents as a sculptor. He had already concocted an image of Ishi that was inane, and not because he was ironic or even surreal, but because he was a retro romantic, you know, a healer dealer in mundane simulations of *indians* as great spirit sculptures. I was courteous over lunch, and less so at the columbarium, but from the very start, not really interested in his work. The idea of the sculpture seemed to be forgotten, but then, out of the granite dust comes this huge lawsuit against me, against Caitlin Croughan, his presumed agent, and the University of California.

ARL: What was the outcome?

GV: Harkin Lucero complained that he had an oral contract to create a sculpture for Ishi Court, and so he sued me, Croughan, and the university for fifty thousand dollars to cover what he claimed to be design and casting costs. This was nonsense, and a nuisance, of course, but nothing could be taken lightly, so we demanded a jury trial. Ishi was there to tease me in court, and he might have been a silent witness in the jury room during deliberations. The verdict, after four days of trial and deliberations, was in my favor, and that was in February 1997. Ishi, no doubt, was not pleased that Lucero had staged his potty spirit show at Mount Olivet Cemetery. Lucero had arranged to have the niche at the columbarium opened, and then, with a newspaper reporter and a video filmmaker present, of course, he lifted the black pot out of the niche. Lucero told me and others at the columbarium that he could feel the spirit of Ishi coming through the pot to his hands, and then his arms, and no doubt, other parts of his body he did not mention.

ARL: This scene is in the play, but was it also evidence in court?

GV: Yes, and the jury watched a video production of that very scene, apparently trying to determine if anyone made him a promise to create a sculpture. Lucero made a rather awkward rubbing of the name and inscription on the pot. The paper was too thick. Ishi would have laughed about such a performance. He was particularly amused, it seemed to me, when the cemetery executive, a young woman, announced that Ishi not only made his own death pot but also carved his own name in the clay. None of this was true, of course, because his preparation for death would have been in visions, songs, and stories, not in pottery. Ishi might have told the experts at the columbarium that he was not a pot maker, and the letters carved on the pot were in a standard typestyle. The sculptor, who claimed to be native, should have known that the inscription on the pot was not a sacred name, not even a native nickname. Ishi was a museum name in Times New Roman, and Lucero, in a mundane gesture, made a rubbing of the name on paper. Here, of course, is yet another retro simulation of names and typestyles.

Zero Larkin, the native sculptor in *Ishi and the Wood Ducks*, raises the rubbing of the name to the camera and the audience.

"Ishi is with me, our spirit is one in his sacred name," says Zero. "I'm going to blast his sacred signature, right from this rubbing, at the bottom of my stone sculpture, my tribute to his power as an Indian." Ishi was in court, the verdict was in my favor, and now he has another story.

5

Discursive Narratives

ARL: In your poetry and in your plays and film scripts you have been dedicated to the notion of upsetting binaries. In your essay "Crows Written on the Poplars: Autocritical Autobiographies" you wrote that "mixedbloods loosen the seams in the shrouds of identities." How has that idea played into your discursive books, *Wordarrows*, *Earthdivers*, and *Crossbloods* in particular?

GV: Yes, most of the characters in my stories outwit, reverse, and overturn the wiles of dominance, and they contradict the simulations of natives. Listen: survivance, the idea of survival and resistance, is more obvious in my stories. So maybe upsetting binaries and resistance are the same as survivance, but a tricky, visionary resistance is more than a structural reversion. I must, however, evade any generalization that would explain my work, certainly my motivation or apparent intentions in stories and discursive essays. Clearly, the seams that need to be loosened were sewn too tightly. The irony here, the cultural irony, is that the seams are simulations of dominance. The seams are sewn over and over by social scientists and other inventors of the American Indian. And the invention is a conservative, national allegory of cultural difference and distinction. The seams get even tighter as more studies are conducted to eliminate all of the loose ends and ambiguities, and to explain every doubt and nuance. The seams are measured right down to the actual words and names in stories about natives. These are the anthroseams, the ironic cultural representations of the other. The great spirit told me to loosen the seams and tease survivance in my name.

ARL: Clement Beaulieu is one of your distant relatives. Why, in your book *Wordarrows: Indians and Whites in the New Fur Trade*, did you choose that name as a persona?

GV: My character is created in the name of a relative to avoid the first person burden. Many of the stories in *Wordarrows* are about my own experience as an advocate in the native community.

I could not bring that much attention to myself, and so my resistance to the first person. Obviously in my autobiography, *Interior Landscapes*, I could not create another name to bear my experiences, but even there, some of my experiences are told by others, as others have seen me at the time.

Robert, the first person is inescapable at times, as you know, and in some narratives there is no better voice. My novel *Dead Voices* is told in the first person, but that voice traces the action, a native shaman who teases the narrator. I am the voice here, in a conversation, but not in a designated category. The author must create the characters and choose the time and form of their voices, and the choices are limited categories.

Gerald Vizenor, the author, seldom uses the "I" even in his own autobiography. I create the "I," but that pronoun is not me, and might even oppose me to others. That single letter does not represent me, but rather it simulates me and teases the reader to hear the pronoun as his own. The "I" is figurative, a transfer of the absence of the author in a pronoun, and the simulated presence of the reader in a first person voice. Clement Beaulieu is my character and reader. I create me as a person in his name, and he is my great uncle and my many selves in stories. I choose that name to avoid the first person pronoun so that the me of my stories is connected to my native family. Many of my stories are not about me but about my experiences, and my activities and experiences were never separations in a pronoun. The stories in *Wordarrows* are told by someone like me, but I must construct that person on the page. Clement Beaulieu was a great storier and he is on the page with me. My persona creates a presence, not a possession. You see, the author, his persona, and his relatives are with me in the book.

ARL: Then, several years later in *Earthdivers: Tribal Narratives on Mixed Descent*, you take aim at what you call "terminal creeds." What are "terminal creeds," and why are they cautionary tales?

GV: Albert Camus and Eric Hoffer had a great influence on me as a college student. Hoffer, the longshoreman and philosopher, published his first book, *The True Believer*, in the early fifties. I first read his book a few years later as a college student. He taught me about ecstatic dominance and mass movements and the fanatic causes of those who believe in the absolute. The notions and simulations of true believers fascinated me, and so, in time, Hoffer's philosophical ideas found their way into my critical interpretation of simulations. My thoughts about the native true believer, and those who truly believe in *indians*, focused on the idea of terminal creeds. Terminal, rather than true, because of federal termination policies and the absence of natives in history, and creed, rather than believer, because of the romantic pursuit of native spiritualism. Eric Hoffer taught me about true believers and fanaticism, and his ideas took shape in my own thoughts about natives and the ambiguities of those who must possess the other by simulations.

ARL: Part of those ambiguities are embodied in the cast of characters that you introduce in *Earthdivers*, such as Captain Shammer, Mouse Proof Martin, Doctor Peter Fountain, Martin Bear Charme, Father Bearald, Rubie Blue Welcome, alongside the wholly literal figures of a Dane Michael White and Thomas White Hawk. This is fact or fiction?

GV: Yes, of course, the characters rush to narrative faction, to fictive journalism, or something like that. The facts are the fiction in *Earthdivers*. You know, the preface to the first edition of *Bearheart* announced that the real names in the novel were not, and the imagined characters were real. Maybe everything is in a name and the simulations are real.

Naturally, the tease of Naanabozho, the *anishinaabe* trickster in stories, was my best teacher in motion, for a time, but the trickster comes to naught, evermore a transmutation, and that was never enough for me. So my stories in *Earthdivers* loosen the seams and outwit the weavers of terminal cultures. That, a trickster hermeneutics, and tease of presence, is my sense of native creation and survivance. My grandmother and uncles teased me in their stories, and later, in college, my sense of presence was touched by Albert Camus, Eric Hoffer, Nikos Kazantzakis, Erich Fromm, and Roland Laing.

ARL: And that carries over into your essays in *Crossbloods*, where you interestingly blend reportage with storytelling, storytelling with reportage. So there is a typical play of meaning in the very title of one of your better-known essays, "Socioacupuncture: Mythic Reversals and the Striptease in Four Acts." In a way, all of these essays are a species of socioacupuncture, are they not?

GV: Maybe they are, and focusing just the right cultural pressure and mediation on the simulations of natives invites the ambiguities of association and meaning. So applying just the right socioacupuncture at the right time can, in stories, heal and liberate.

ARL: The very form of your essays, and the form of your witness, is a literary interplay of identity, terminal creeds, and history. So two things come together. One loosens the seams in terms of your historical and cultural interpretations, and also loosens the seams in the ways you choose to write about these "crossblood" inheritances?

GV: Listen, that holds together too much of an abstract, categorical association of the work. I must resist any easy reference to crossbloods, as if that combined word and metaphor were a recognizable entity. The cross and the blood are unnameable. The tease of a crossblood presence in native histories is over the simulation of a seam, a double seam, as you suggest, of established poses, appearances, interpretations, and loose assertions of identity.

ARL: Would "narrative chance," one of your signature title phrases, hold for the essays in your book *Manifest Manners: Postindian Warriors of Survivance?* What of narrative chance and survivance?

GV: Yes, survivance is a narrative chance. *Manifest Manners* starts with the chance of two exotic journeys. Meriwether Lewis and William Clark needed natives on their expedition. In other words, they were not scared by the presence of natives. Rather, they were haunted by their absence. Luther Standing Bear, several generations later, was on an expedition in the other direction. He was one of the first natives to graduate from the federal Carlisle Indian School in Pennsylvania. He needed the other to learn the manifest manners of dominance, because he and other natives had became a simulation, an absence. Standing Bear, Lewis, and Clark created their own ironic presence in the book. Narrative chance teases that sense of a literary presence, that chance to summon any name, to scare, and to create in stories more than another terminal creed by mere victimry. Even in the most isolated acts of imagination a writer must create a language game of time, people, places, and seasons, and tease the obvious associations of history. The author must create a new bundle of metaphors in stories so that a narrative chance might be a presence in the book.

ARL: Gerald, *Manifest Manners* certainly begins with a tease on the very cover. You have taken an Andy Warhol silk screen portrait of Russell Means about which your text says, "This is not an Indian." How did that come about?

GV: The tease, as you know, is inspired by René Magritte's painting "This is not a pipe." The idea is that a certain image, a word, a name, a simulation can take the place of the real. So the Warhol portrait of Russell Means on the cover of *Manifest Manners* is an ironic simulation, and surely a pricey tease might be, "This is not an Indian." There is a double irony and an allegorical absence of natives in the portrait. The *indian* is a discoverable museum absence. Clearly the stoical image of the warrior is one simulation, and the other ironic simulation is that the actual artistic production of the silk screen was only supervised by Andy Warhol. Means, the warrior image, is teased by the absence of the artist and natives, teased by line and color. Warhol was ironic about soup cans and luminaries, and he must have been saying, "This is not an Indian."

ARL: Obviously, the title *Manifest Manners* plays on the phrase "manifest destiny." The manifest is clear in the context of cultural dominance, but why the manner in manifest?

GV: Robert, cultural dominance was the manifest, and now manners is the disguise of destiny. The manifest was overturned by resistance, casinos, lawsuits, conceit, and countersimulations – otherwise natives would be the eternal creatures of victimry. Not everyone recognizes that in the notion of manifest destiny, but surely most people have a general understanding, at least from the movies, that some adventurous destiny, cruel and unusual, ended out west, and out back, and now we have a nation of casinos, manifest manners, and affirmative action. The manifest has been revised, but the notions of an originary national history are the new manners of destiny.

Dare we say that manifest manners are postmonotheistic? Dare we declare that binary structures of good and evil, savagism and civilization, have ended? Dare we declare an end to the binary structures of gender? Dare we say that racial enlightenment has removed the mark of the other and manifest destiny? Maybe, someone might say, but every response, rhetorical or not, must be ironic and cynical. The *indian* is the absence. Natives are the presence, but manifest manners court the *authentic* evidence of absence, the romance of ethnic dioramas and cultural simulations. Natives continue to be bound by manifest manners in the literary arts, in popular culture, and history. Andy Warhol must have measured the conceit of a simulation by the celebration of his creations, and so he might have said, to tease the scarcity and market price of his simulations even more, "This has never been an Indian."

ARL: You suggest, then, that the Indian is better termed postindian. How did that come about? What do you mean by "postindian"?

GV: The *indian* is the absence, natives the presence, and an absence because the name is a discoverable, and a historical simulation of distinct native cultures. Columbus warred, scored, rocked, talked, and coveted the other, and so we come around five centuries later to say, You made a mistake, and how ironic your discovery. Surely, five centuries as a discoverable is enough of victimry. Casino politics is the game now, and the romantic, tragic poses of the *indian* are not as convincing as they were a decade ago. Yes, the pose of the natural ecologist endures, but most natives are wiser to the simulations. The point is that we are long past the colonial invention of the *indian*. We come after the invention, and we are the postindians. That says more about who we are not, which is significant in identity politics, and nothing about who we are or might become as postindians. Natives, of course, use simulations too, but for reasons of liberation rather than dominance. Postindians create a native presence, and that sense of presence is both reversion and futurity. Yes, and the reversions are tricky and ironic, as they have always been in native stories, but never so easy as cultural victimry.

  I wrote the word *indian* in italics and lower case throughout the text of my first book of essays, *The Everlasting Sky: New Voices from the People Named the Chippewa*. I pointed out in the introduction that the noun, a simulation, printed in italics, should constantly remind the reader that *indian* is a casual, and later calculated, colonial name. I wrote, about thirty years ago, "Before you begin listening to the *oshki anishinaabe* speaking in this book, please write a short definition of the word *indian*. Your brief organization of thoughts about the word *indian* will help you understand the problems of identity among tribal people who are burdened with names invented by the dominant society." The *anishinaabe*, as you know, bear variations of the names Chippewa and Ojibway. My point is that the native word *oshki* means "new," or "the first time," and so *oshki anishinaabe* is my postindian name for the new natives of the vast woodland area of the western Great Lakes.

ARL: Postindian is your conception, and is the word a way, too, of calling up Jean Baudrillard's theories of simulation, the absolute fake?

GV: Well, it is, by chance and invention. The *indian* is the invention, and *indian* cultures are simulations, that is, the ethnographic construction of a model that replaces the real in most academic references. Natives are the real, the ironies of the real, and an unnameable sense of presence, but simulations are the absence, and so the *indian* is an absence, not a presence. You see, *indians* are simulations of the discoverable other, and only posers or the naive dare stand with that ironic name. That is to say, the simulations of the other have no real origin, no original reference, and there is no real place on this continent that bears the meaning of that name. The *indian* was simulated to be an absence, to be without a place. The reference of the simulation is a weak metaphor of colonialism and, of course, manifest manners.

The postindian is after the simulation, and the sense of a native presence is both resistance and survivance. So the presence of postindians teases the reader to see the absence, the simulation of the other, as a problem. Natives seldom speak to each other as simulations, except as a tricky tease of dominance, but natives are burdened with five centuries of inventions and ethnographic simulations of their absence. The postindian stands for an active, ironic resistance to dominance, and the good energy of native survivance.

ARL: Would that postindian notice come to a focus in a film like *Dances with Wolves?* That is, the simulation of a romantic pose?

GV: Yes, *Dances with Wolves* is about dirty dancing with horses, nature, a vast landscape, and of course, the bright natives of the prairie. Dunbar, the cavalry officer, rides out of a warrior tradition with a white woman and leaves the tragic natives to their fate. That must be a postindian simulation, you see, because the warriors are heroic, and a white woman is there, no doubt, to prove the revisions of that popular structural theme of savagism and civilization. She seems bettered by the touch of natives, contrary to most stories of captivity. I might say something like that about the simulations of natives in several other movies that clearly celebrate a postwestern reversion of naturalism, idealism, and a curious fascination with traditional authenticity. The postindian simulations in these movies are radical turns of savagism, a romantic resistance at best, and seem to serve terminal creeds. I wonder if these scenes of simulated traditions are not, once again, the mythic adventures of a nation worried about violence and the corruption of the environment, and, we might wonder, if these revisions of *indian* simulations are traces of fascism.

Consider the movie *Little Big Man*, with Chief Dan George and Dustin Hoffman. Here, for the first time in movies, we see natives with a sense of irony about history. Yet the story is about a naive white boy who gives a more generous meaning to the absence of natives. The postindian simulations show the natives dressed to the traditional nines, wise and noble, always daring and inspired about nature, the weather, and their communities. The simulations of survivance are in the reversal of savagism and civilization, to such an extent that it is difficult to remember a decent white character in either *Little Big Man* or *Dances with Wolves*. And of course, we know the end, the tragic end of the wise warriors. The end, in spite of the romantic reversals of savagism, holds to a tragic mode, the imitation of action that arouses strong emotions in the audience. At last, and at the end of the movie reversions, the *indians* are storied back to an absence, not a presence in history. Simulations are neither good nor bad, but are masks with nothing behind them. Postindian simulations are another kind of mask that obscures the real. So there are postindian simulations in these movies, but what, in a mythic sense, are these movies about? Natives on the screen are, at last, much better than ever, but soldiers are the new savages in postwestern movies. Someone, no doubt, is eager to produce *Dances with Casinos*, a postindian movie satire of treaties, avarice, envies, and countervictimry.

ARL: Even though many of the native actors were Sioux, the original Michael Blake novel was supposedly Comanche. That really compounds that irony, does it not?

GV: Listen, that suggests some sort of tradition of simulations. *Dances with Wolves* is a very tricky conversion of savagism and civilization. The ironies, it seems to me, are twice earned in every scene, as the simulations of natives in the novel are outdistanced by others in the movie. Surely, in the great tradition of postindian movie posers, someone must honor the actors Jay Silverheels, Iron Eyes Cody, and Russell Means.

ARL: Would you extend that equally to the latest film version of *The Last of the Mohicans*, and the return of Russell Means?

GV: Russell Means is one of the most bankable postindian movie actors and – whatever, say variationative, an assertive, original simulator of native traditions – ever to hang around the movie commissaries. He's a strong man, never weak, and since he moved from radical politics to movie sets, he has never titled to victimry. Means turns simulations into contracts, and at the same time, he poses as a warrior of authenticity. Means is a native by blood, family, and community, but he is also a character in the tricky theater of variationative poses. A "great sickness is coming," he warned the world in his recent autobiography, *Where White Men Fear to Tread*. What sickness would that be, the movies? How does he know our futurity, by shamanic ecstasies, or by some postindian confluence of movies? Maybe he already has some ghost at work on his first celebrity novel.

ARL: Presumably, you would also include in that Paula Gunn Allen's concern about aliens and interest in channeling through a crystal skull?

GV: Yes, now that is a fantastic journey she poses in her work on channeling, something about the course of unnameable energy in the aesthetic form of a polished crystal skull. Her story is strong, and quite extraordinary. My ambition is to tease the same tricky channels on a crystal set, and hear Crystal Woman singing a show tune, the pure simulation of a crystal head of originary culture. I might lower my voice in turn and sing along in a crystal state.

ARL: Turning to a more consequential issue, you took exception to *The Broken Cord* by Louise Erdrich and the late Michael Dorris for the ways in which they perpetuate, willingly or otherwise, the great firewater myth in their activities and their activism over Fetal Alcohol Syndrome.

GV: Michael Dorris wrote about adoption and the *indian* disease named Fetal Alcohol Syndrome. Obviously, there is no such racial, cultural, or genetic syndrome, but the stereotype of drunken *indians* has always been part of the separatists' myths of savagism and civilization. The title of his book is a terminal metaphor, and an invitation, it seems to me, to aesthetic re-morse and tragic victimry. That single stereotype, the drunken *indian*, has outlasted any other in the curious course of scientific studies and cultural dominance. Dorris worries over his adopted children, and he shares his love, pain, and humor as a parent. So his personal narrative has touched many readers, but the reader is not innocent and must come to this book with many simulations. Indeed, *The Broken Cord* separates *indian* alcoholic abuse from a wider consideration. The narrow focus is a tragic closure. The tone of the book is victimry. Some readers, strongly influenced by the story, might resist the selection of a native child at the moment of fosterage or adoption. The ordinary troubles of children, or even an honorable adolescent resistance, could be seen as Fetal Alcohol Syndrome.

I was a child put out to fosterage, and wonder now, given what many people believe about *indians*, if some of my behavior at the time might have been seen as the inheritance of heavy drinkers. Dorris clearly intended to inform readers of a serious problem, and to bear witness, as he does so painfully, to the behavior of an adopted son and the characteristics of Fetal Alcohol Syndrome. Listen, this is a terrible, haunting story in the tragic mode, and all the more tragic since the suicide of Michael Dorris.

Yes, and then the politics of readers, the private turns and emotive manners, beget another cause, the real possibility that some children available for adoption might live out a silent, mean exclusion because of this book, *The Broken Cord*. That silence, of course, would be a terrible closure, but obviously never so devastating as the actual consequences of being poisoned by alcohol. Native children must bear so many cruelties caused by beverage alcohol, a poison, a party, fosterage, abuse, loneliness, and maybe another separation by scientific studies and adoption stories.

ARL: Consider "Double Others," the second essay in *Manifest Manners*. Is that what leads you to show the degree of sympathy you do for one of the first known native medical doctors, Charles Alexander Eastman, and his reaction to what occurred at Wounded Knee?

GV: The Wounded Knee massacre was an act of racial vengeance by cavalry soldiers. Charles Eastman, who had just completed his medical training, arrived as the first native doctor on the Pine Ridge Reservation only a few months before the massacre. That experience, treating the few survivors, changed his worldview. The story of that horror worries me now, so imagine how natives were pained at the time.

Luther Standing Bear, for instance, wrote about how difficult it was for him to continue teaching the virtues of civilization. He worried that the soldiers had no respect for women or children. He was one of the first graduates of the Carlisle Indian School and had returned to the reservation a short time before the massacre. Eastman and Standing Bear were never the same, and after the massacre they both became writers. They must have understood that natives would survive in the book. Maybe their memories of that horror were variations of post-traumatic stress syndrome. They were burdened by the memories of the massacre, and the consequences of such emotional experiences must be similar to the violence and horrors of the Vietnam War.

Eastman took up writing as a way to reach a larger audience. He wrote that natives were a noble people, and later he became a consultant to various national organizations to teach the wisdom and spirit of natives and their cultures. Now, of course, many people look upon him as romantic, and somewhat simplistic because he wrote to young people. My view is that the context of his traumatic experiences must be read into every scene of his stories. He was dedicated to teach the nation about the honor, the rich soul of native people, and the survivance of native communities, but not violence or victimry.

ARL: Yes, "honor, the rich soul of native people." The chapter that follows in *Manifest Manners*, "Shadow Survivance," in turn takes a shot at the role of anthropology in understanding the cultures of Native Americans. Why have you been so fierce in the views you have entertained about anthropology?

GV: I have not been fierce enough about anthropology. There are no measures of fierceness that could be reparations for the theft of native irony, humor, and original stories. There's not enough time to be critical of the academic enterprise of cultural anthropology. This work that plagues every native in the universe is despicable; it's only in the interests of profits and power that these studies and simulations of culture are given institutional authority. Cultural anthropologists pose with their booty, and universities honor these academic predators with advanced degrees, and then they go out to create even more anthropologists to study natives and others around the world. Imagine that injustice in the name of higher education and academic ethics. Consider the arrogance of a culture that believes in outside experts, the experts who create simulations, and consider a culture that believes in such experts over natives, over the wit and wisdom of native stories, and the cultural predators who reduce the original, mythic, and ironic perceptions of natives to mere material evidence. Consider the cruelty of a culture that converts native reason and tricky stories into dumbwaiter theories and celebrates museum simulations over a native presence. Who are these agents of manifest manners? Well, none other than anthropologists with no culture of their own.

ARL: And yet cultural anthropologists often cast themselves in the rather pitiless role of "the friend of the Indian."

GV: So you ask about that culture set, the one that even rescues natives, of course, because the academic actors have so many masks – as one corners, another rescues, and the academic service continues – but the set, the stony set, must rescue their own simulations. What else do they have to rescue? Set anthropologists rescue the discoverable other, never themselves, and yet these apologists carry out the separatism of the social science. They could do much better to rescue themselves from the manifest manners of academic institutions, but that, surely, would reveal an empty mask.

ARL: Do you see this being challenged in part by your editorship of the American Indian Literature and Critical Studies Series at the University of Oklahoma Press, and by friends and contemporaries like Thomas King, Louis Owens, and even Elizabeth Cook-Lynn? Do you see, as it were, a body of literature that challenges some of these methods, some of these systems, which have come out of the social sciences?

GV: Native American literature is much more than a challenge to the social sciences, as you know; it is liberation, and a visionary sovereignty. Native literature is an act of survivance. Some native writers, however, create a tighter seam of tradition in their stories, as if they are reaching for an authority outside their own creation. Such a reach for tradition and authority, and without a sense of irony, sounds to me like a terminal creed, when in fact we should liberate ourselves by imagination rather than substituting one methodology for another.

ARL: Speaking of imaginative liberation, a figure who has interested you and about whom you have frequently written is the great high admiral himself, Christopher Columbus. You have been at pains to show how we've not sufficiently imagined him in his complexity. Why is he so significant?

GV: So many people in the past five centuries have given such careful thought to the adventures and experiences of this figure in history. Figure indeed, and yet there are many stories not told about his cruise. How extraordinary that his mission was tied to the discovery of precious minerals. Columbus was a slaver, a warmonger, a man without much humor who was tricked by many natives, and who was never paid the tithe due on his discoveries. The Spanish government, it seems to me, should actually pay natives the tithe, with interest, once due the explorer. So natives, in this sense, are the discoverable heirs of that original agreement.

Christopher Columbus is a tricky liberation story. His adventures are matters of great irony. Who, after five centuries, could turn his absence into victimry? Many, many natives, that's who, and with much attention by the media. I am always amazed at how elaborate are the structures of victimry. This may be a good time, once more, to declare that Columbus was native. Yes, he was adopted by shamans, in much the same way politicians are adopted at election time, and the proof is in the gift of a headdress. Columbus was one of the very first postindian adoptees, and since then the heirs have told so many tricky stories in his name.

Stephen Greenblatt, in *Marvelous Possessions*, observes Columbus in that great exploration show, the discovery of others and the marvelous, and so constructed by land and sea, teased forever by the creation of the other, the wondrous other in the distance of documents and narratives. Columbus, of course, is my very other; the lost and lonesome native is one more marvelous story. Columbus, you see, was returning to his native homeland with a western gaze, and that should be evidence enough to recover the tithe in his name.

ARL: The homeland that you have him come back to in your novel *The Heirs of Columbus* is not some unidimensional fifteenth century but a place inhabited by contemporary modern and postmodern Native Americans. And that brings up casinos. You created the title "Casino Coups" for your essay in *Manifest Manners*. Columbus to casinos — who are the players now?

GV: Casinos are a tricky coup, a postindian coup, that touch of a winner at a technical distance. Stone Columbus is the tricky casino native in my novel *The Heirs of Columbus* who funds a new native nation with casino cash and heals wounded children, the heirs of a chemical civilization. My stories, as you know, tease the posers, court ambiguities, loosen the seams of tradition, and release a healing energy, or an energy that might heal in the mind of a good reader. And all of that comes about in the novel by the riches won or lost by others at casinos. That works easily in fiction, the stories of luck and chance and fear and loss and the play and apology of the great spirits that influence slot machines. Casino stories might even cure the modern conceit of traditions. Well, casinos have distracted the lost and lonesome, and with some humor, but not with a native vision that heals. How ironic that native chance is over at casinos, and the cash is a measure of political envy. The treaty promises of native sovereignty were never bankable.

"Casino Coups," my critical essay about casinos in *Manifest Manners*, considers the causes of envy, and the inevitable sacrifice of native sovereignty to casino games. Not chance, but the will to lose money on a reservation. Hannah Arendt argued in *Antisemitism* that wealth without power is a cause of hate and envy.

Many reservation casinos are rich, gross, and powerless, and these combinations invite the envies of racists and politicians, not to mention the inspired hatred of separatists and patriots. So the envies of casinos could be the end of native sovereignty. My worries are over that moment when traditionalists and the religious right come together to curse the sins of casino gambling in native communities. That envy will probably be the most difficult and painful challenge to sovereignty. My concern is that a generation of very bright natives could run with the cash, as a shine of postindian rights and reparations, and only agonize the politics of envy and native sovereignty. The Supreme Court might hear a case over taxation on treaty land, the rights of states and native casinos, and rule against the idea of native sovereignty.

ARL: At the end of your epilogue to *Manifest Manners* you embrace a number of the issues you call "survivance hermeneutics." You write, "Postindian narratives are suspensive; the shadows, and presence of tribal traditions, have no hierarchies in libraries, because interpretations are signatures of imagination and the liberation of narratives. These are not the binaries of savagism and civilization; rather, the paradoxes of narrative fear, the suspension of domination, and survivance hermeneutics." What do you mean by narrative survivance?

GV: Natives must create a narrative presence in the book, as you know, otherwise the shadows of our names, and stories of nicknames, and even the visions of shamans are taken over by manifest manners. Survivance, in my use of the word, means a native sense of presence, the motion of sovereignty and the will to resist dominance. Survivance is not just survival but also resistance, not heroic or tragic, but the tease of tradition, and my sense of survivance outwits dominance and victimry.

Survival is a response; survivance is a standpoint, a worldview, and a presence. Yes, and there is a sense of dependency in the meaning of the word *survival*, a dependency on the cause of some action. *Dominance* is a strong word and stands for the historical prominence of such conditions. Many natives are experts on the nuances of dominance, and most histories of natives are themes of dominance and victimry. My stories are about survivance, not victimry. So survivance is resistance and hermeneutics.

6

Bearheart Chronicles

ARL: You made your literary bow as a novelist with *Darkness in Saint Louis Bearheart*, which was first published in 1978. You revised that novel twelve years later and retitled it *Bearheart: The Heirship Chronicles*. What led to the change of title?

GV: Most people referred to my first novel as *Bearheart* long before the title was changed. Others remembered my novel as *Darkness* or *Saint Louis*, and obviously had some difficulty finding it in bookstores. So it made perfect sense to change the title to *Bearheart*, one strong word, in the later edition published by the University of Minnesota Press. The subtitle, *The Heirship Chronicles*, comes out of the fact that the novel is inside a narrative written by Saint Louis Bearheart, who worked most of his life in the heirship division, or as a young radical said, "the hairship," of the Bureau of Indian Affairs in Washington. The novel begins there, in a federal heirship office, where Bearheart, an old man, gestures to a young radical to find the manuscript of his novel in a file cabinet. The subtitle is a reference to the actual novel written by the man named Bearheart.

ARL: So, in a way, and right from the start of Bearheart, the novel is a message in a bottle, a postindian text written within a text?

GV: Yes, but the first version of *Bearheart* was not within a text. The first draft of my novel began, in fact, in the office of the omniscient narrator who observed everything. I wrote most of the novel in the voice of an older native man, the first draft, and realized the need for some other introduction to the scenes. The problem was the wild content and action of the novel demanded too much from the omniscient narrator, as it was first written, and readers would surely think of me as the narrator and author rather than an older man, a tricky shaman who was an employee of the federal government. Someone else had to create the narrative of *Bearheart*. The narrator had to be a native shaman, a visionary. Bearheart created his chronicle over the many years he worked in the heirship division of the Bureau of Indian Affairs. Franz Kafka created stories about the mundane contradictions of bureaucracies, the cracks and paranoid tragedies of nuisance service. Bearheart creates stories out of his visions, the myths of solace, and the fantastic violence of futurity. He wrote his novel at the end of gasoline and civilization.

ARL: Bearheart's vision takes the form of a quest in which Proude Cedarfair, who is a ceremonial bear, and a company of pilgrims travel from the headwaters of the Mississippi River to Chaco Canyon in New Mexico. In what sense did you have in your mind some of the older pilgrimage stories, Dante, Chaucer, or Bunyan?

GV: My first consideration was a conversion of the themes of discovery, western expansion, and manifest destiny. Proude Cedarfair and a circus of native pilgrims were driven to the road because the country ran out of gasoline and the economy crashed overnight. Bearheart is on a native journey, a reversal of that western movement. Pilgrimages and the tease of traditions are not new, of course, in oral stories or literary history. The stories of motion, survivance, and sovereignty are common in narratives everywhere. I did not want to make so much out of removal or expulsion or dominance. Removal was one episode, and the other stories in the novel are in motion, on the road without gasoline. Natives come alive in stories on the road, on an ironic pilgrimage, but not in carrying out some mundane objection to manifest manners. My *Bearheart* is a survivance pilgrimage, and so are the stories in *The Canterbury Tales*.

ARL: Louis Owens writes in *Other Destinies* that "Bearheart is a post-apocalyptic allegory of mixedblood pilgrim clowns afoot in a world gone predictably mad." The journey of the characters in Bearheart is as much across contemporary as ancestral America. How did these postindian ironies come to mind?

GV: Naturally, as the journey is the sovereignty of motion – and once again, the stories are survivance, not victimry. My novel is heat and irony, not a heroic imitation of action, and the politics of identity is too whiny and mundane to run with the tricky motion of native stories. *Bearheart* is a journey of survivance at the end of a chemical civilization, a wild cut of presence, and the consequences of this material failure, long after waves of righteous immigrants, mercenary settlements, mining, the simulations of postwestern movies, and the exclusion and removal of natives, are new shamanic ecstasies. Bearheart, the old man who wrote this novel as an heirship clerk, envisioned a constitutional democracy that turned to racial violence as the nation ran out of gasoline. Once more natives were on a dangerous road, a pilgrimage on the interstates, and everywhere gangs ruled the rest stops. The reader, it seemed to me at the time, had to be convinced that the end of civilization was as calculated as it had been at the start. So the descriptive scenes of violence were ironic, allegories of the many massacres of natives. Every rest stop on the interstate was a Wounded Knee or a Sand Creek. The scenes, of course, are trickster cuts and transformations, and the stories tease the allegories in *Pilgrim's Progress*, or even *Moby Dick*.

The descriptive violence in *Bearheart* is both material and ironic because civilization is the cost of gasoline. In other words, the culture was held together by a dependence on chemicals, and when the gasoline ran out, that was the end of civilization, otherwise the agents of peace would not have turned to violence. Tragedy was aesthetic, but everyone has been teased to death by murder in the movies, and at the end it was violence that ruled the rest stops on the interstates, the banal imitations of human cruelties. Natives were no strangers to separatism, removal, and violence in the name of civilization, and so, on the road, and at the rest stops, natives carried on their tricky stories. People with terminal creeds and no sense of irony were forever wounded, not only by the end of gasoline and civilization, but also by their dependence on evangelism and television. Natives have always been in motion, on the road, in trickster stories, and so the allegories are natural reason in *Bearheart*.

ARL: America, then, is out of oil and spiritual balance?

GV: Indeed, and so the violence is allegorical. I started the novel at the time the country experienced a petroleum shortage and there were long lines and violent encounters at service stations. Daily there were stories in the newspapers about the violence. I waited in line more than once with the fuel gauge on empty. Yes, the nation was out of spiritual balance and common prayers never seemed to change the transportation system. Way back, fifty years ago, my first date with a girl was carried out by electric streetcar, not by automobile. We sat on wicker seats, ate licorice, and then the oil barons bought the streetcars and sold me on cars.

ARL: And the pilgrims head toward Chaco Canyon, an ancient native place, to enter the fourth world. What is the tribal fourth world?

GV: The world of imagination, transformation, and survivance. But actually, the number four in the way of the worlds depends on the time, place, and native creation story. Bearheart, the old man, envisions the fourth world, a season of creation and transmutation, and a world of shamanic journeys and visionary survivance. The fourth world is in the stories of animals, and an instance of other lives at other times. Stories are the creation, and the fourth world is a creation story.

ARL: The fourth world is renewal, a world of spiritual revitalization?

GV: Yes, and the stories of creation are survivance, as the creation takes place in the performance of the story. Not a comment on creation, and not a reduction, but a sense of a native presence in the telling of the story. In other words, the creation takes place in the story. Natives are created in stories, and natives have always been on the road to revitalization. The Ghost Dance religion is a good story of revitalization, and the stories of the dance were told widely by the first graduates of federal boarding schools. The irony is that a revitalization movement was learned in the language of dominance. There is an energy of this vision and dance that is part of the motion of sovereignty, a spiritual journey. That energy has always been present in native consciousness, visions, and stories.

ARL: You have this wondrous plumage in the names of characters in your novel. Proude Cedarfair, for instance. What of his name?

GV: Cedar is sacred and cedar heals; sacred in mode and manner of stories in natural scenes. The bark is richly scented, and to burn cedar is to create a sacred presence, to transform the moment, the senses, and memories. Cedar smoke balances an otherwise dangerous world.

ARL: And Cedarfair Circus?

GV: Circus in the sense of clowns, and circus as a circle, a native circus, a cedar circus of visionary clowns and trickster crows. The word is language play and amusement, and a good metaphor to name a circle of visionary natives on a journey. The circus pilgrims are a tricky circle of animals and birds, mongrels and crows. The circus is a continuous performance too, the play of animals and tricksters on the road to the fourth world.

ARL: Then there's the prodigious Benito Saint Plumero, or Bigfoot, and his enormous penis named President Jackson. You obviously had a lot of fun in creating this figure.

GV: Bigfoot – you mean his prodigious dick with an ironic nickname of President Jackson. Trickster stories, as you know, create many wild encounters with dicks, enormous dicks, gigantic dicks too much for even a trickster to bear. Some stories have the trickster with a dick so big he topples over when it goes erect, or the story of a lost dick, or a dick eaten by fish. Bigfoot, an ironic nickname suggestive of the size of his dick, is also known as Double Saint.

Bigfoot, a mongrel with sexual fantasies, visits the Scapehouse on Callus Road, a sanctuary of sensitive women located near the reservation in northern Minnesota. Saint Louis Bearheart writes that the "thirteen weird and sensitive women have never known a chief executive to stand so tall and last so long and to be so proud as President Jackson. It was not uncommon for six or seven scapehouse poets to spend the long nights lusting with the namesake president." So we have the natural tease of trickster stories, a giant dick, the allegory of a chief executive who stuck it to natives, and then we have the pleasurable secondary immediacy of the ironic postindian dick on a pilgrimage of survivance and sovereignty.

ARL: Who is Bishop Omax Parasimo?

GV: Bishop Omax Parasimo, a cleric on the wicked road in my novel *Bearheart*. He carries three metamasks in a black case, a priest of many curious poses. The creation of his surname turns on the name of one of my very best friends, Jerry Gerasimo. I first met him in the middle of the block on his way to an education conference sponsored by the Bureau of Indian Affairs in Minneapolis. I admired his polished boots and determined gait, and advised him not to attend the conference. So we talked for two hours about the film *Easy Rider*. Gerasimo, his wife, Dorothy, and their three daughters took me into their family. Several months later he invited me to apply for a teaching position at Lake Forest College. That was in the late sixties, a time of many nicknames, poses, and metamasks. Gerasimo is a great teacher, a storier of bears, rivers, and winters at Lake Namakan.

We tease each other by names, and so the bishop of meta-masks, beyond Gerasimo. I imagined his great stories on the road, the turn of faces, the wild humor, his acts of mercy, and every gesture a tricky sense of presence. Once, in a marvelous contest of imagination, we played marbles with native children during recess at a remote mission boarding school in Manitoba, Canada. We played against the gestures and situational images of each other, and the children were so eager to share the ordinary union of our native tease. His father might have known my father. Our fathers died so young, and now we have become their stories.

ARL: And who is Lilith Mae Farrier?

GV: Lilith Mae Farrier is a friend only in a literary road story. She plays out various historical antecedents, to be sure, but she is a character of my creation. She is a farrier of horses, a dead letter linear thinker, and a profoundly conscientious teacher on the reservation. She is dedicated to the pragmatic manners of education, to an ironic fault, and that fault is her isolation, and so, out of difference and loneliness, she carries on with the love of animals, the wild intimacy of two brownish boxer dogs. Here is the play on native stories of human and animal relations, the wild allegories, ironies, and myths of families. The stories tease a native creation, a time of stones and tricksters, a time when humans and animals and birds got on pretty well, including language, and sex, and in some of the best native stories humans were related to bears, the creation of crossbloods. So the stories of human and animal unions created the first crossblood bears, wolves, eagles, and other creatures. Later, in *Bearheart*, that tricky union is between a reservation teacher and boxer dogs.

Lilith Mae Farrier, by name and practice, is a creation of animal love, lust, and family. Such memories of transformational stories, or stories of associations with other life forms, were common, not surprising, and in fact, continue to be familiar native stories. I play out the pleasure of animal myths in the story of a contemporary white schoolteacher who lives with two boxers on the reservation. The play of this myth has caused some readers to accuse me of native perversity, and some have turned on me with anger over the erotic act of humans and animals in *Bearheart*. I have been faulted, and publicly in some cases, for being so crude and rude as to associate women with the sexual intimacies of bears and dogs. Not only that, but a group of natives once shunned me because I told a story at a conference about how bears masturbate. They seemed to be more troubled by the act of masturbation in general than by bears alone. That conservative avoidance, no doubt, was some fateful curse of missionaries. Luckily, the bears were spared the missions.

Naturally, my response to accusations of literary perversity must be a totemic irony. I said, "Are you against nature and native stories, and is there something wrong with loving an animal?" I find nothing wrong in the love of an animal, and I find nothing wrong in the sexual associations between animals, especially in the creation of a trickster story. There's more to gain than lose in the love of animals. And my novel is one of those stories. Even more to the point, so to speak, is the erotic theme of monastic masturbation with animals in "Headwaters Curiosa," the last story in my novel *Hotline Healers*. Lilith Mae lived much longer and was much happier with two boxers than she would have been with men. She was teased by natives, healed by animals, and she died by fire.

ARL: Another figure is Inawa Biwide. Where does that name come from? How did you conceive of his role in your novel?

GV: Inawa Biwide, the stranger, is a bird and a bear vision at the end of the stories in *Bearheart*. He learned to see as a bird, one eye at a time, and at a great distance. Biwide was on the road with Proude Cedarfair, Pure Gumption, the mongrel, and of course with the crows and other pilgrims in *Bearheart*. At the end of the novel he moved in magical flight over the pueblo, out of the ruins with the sun of the winter solstice. There were bear tracks in the snow, and the novel ends with laughter, "the old men laughed and laughed and told stories about changing woman and visions bears."

Inawa Biwide is a sacred name, a native nickname. He lives at the edge of silence, an orphan once rescued by the church, and at age sixteen he joined the ceremony of the pilgrims, mongrels, and crows on the road to a mythic survivance. Bishop Parasimo is his tricky master, a man who wears many metamasks. The word *biiwide* in *anishinaabe* means a visitor or stranger, and his first name is an obscure word noted in the Baraga *Dictionary of the*

Otchipwe Language. The word *inawa* means "similar to someone," or a resemblance. So in *Bearheart* his native name is visionary and means "the one who resembles a stranger." He moves above harm, at a natural escape distance in silence, and seems to be immune to violence and victimry.

ARL: As you take the pilgrims through the various episodes, you also show a very special affection for crows and the dogs, especially Pure Gumption and Private Jones. Such affection for animals is common in your writing, but you show a particular fondness and intimacy for these two dogs. Why are they central characters?

GV: Robert, my affection is obvious. You are talking to the mongrel in me. I was born a dog. So these are stories about my relatives. Take a good look at me, and then look at early photographs of me. Look closely and you can see the dog in me as a child, and as a young man. And then in later photographs you might begin to wonder, what ever happened to that dog? There he is, a mongrel on his route as a paper boy, delivering daily newspapers and running with the dogs, and there, in that photograph, the mongrel is riding his new bicycle. And then, by the time of my graduation from college, standing there in that photograph with my stupid mongrel smile, and wearing that ridiculous black gown, you might notice a new disguise. But the dog is there, caught in the smile, in the cock of the head, teased in a vision, and noticed by the paw. The dog in me took up the pen to write stories about my ancestors. Private Jones, as you know, was eaten by soldiers in *Bearheart.* Pure Gumption, Admire, Chicken Lips, Hawk, Casino Rose, Agate Eyes, and many other great mongrels are in my most recent book, *Hotline Healers.* My mongrel relatives, in fact, are graduates of a driving school on the reservation. They are the most loyal chauffeurs. You see, my imagination runs with the tricky mongrels. I am a graduate of that same driving school. Maybe we have always been on this wild canine journey.

ARL: Eventually in their travels in the hyperreality of a civilization without gasoline, the pilgrims meet the evil gambler. Does this evil gambler come out of your own experience?

GV: Naturally, but do you mean racial politics?

ARL: Yes, but also from your interest in myth and fable?

GV: The evil gambler is here, at the table. Choose a gender, turn a story, and there is an evil gambler. The evil gambler is a universal metaphor, a great demon of wind and mountain, a natural figuration of terror, of the unknown, the fear of death, but the evil gambler is much wiser than the monotheistic devil and his banal body fires. Native evil is a game, and we are the gamblers of survivance. Evil is at the sides, over the mountains, on high side and lows, out of sight, and the center is never a balance because the center is a manner, not a game. So the native shamans and tricksters might say, always hold one eye on evil and stay with the game. Everyone must play the games of the evil gambler, and the best players are always thinking about the game. The games are on the dark side, and we are the lonesome players. My father, you know, lost the game in the city.

The *anishinaabe* told trickster stories about the great evil gambler who lived over the mountains in the west, a place that has always been outside of ordinary time. Native evil is beyond the pleasurable memories of a journey. In trickster stories the natives who played with the evil gambler lost their hands, arms, body parts, and heart in the game. Few natives ever returned from the games, but those who did told about the hideous, wicked laughter of the evil gambler.

The first *anishinaabe* grandmother, Nookomis, teased and warned her grandson, the trickster Naanabozho, never to travel in the land of hideous humans over the mountains, and never give in to the temptation of the evil gambler. Naturally, the trickster was determined to outwit the evil gambler, and that is a metaphor that gives meaning to many native stories today. Curiously, there was no wise *anishinaabe* grandfather, or Nimishoomis, in these first oral stories of the trickster. Our Nimishoomis was already on the great road at the time of creation looking for a new game. Sir Cecil Staples, the monarch of unleaded gasoline, is the evil gambler in *Bearheart*. Proude Cedarfair is Nimishoomis, the grandfather, and he beats the evil gambler in a game for gasoline. Sir Staples wheezed and drooled over the native dish game. The players crack the dish and count the number of wooden figures that remain standing. Cedarfair teased the wind, and he was good at that, and the figures wobbled and fell over in the dish. Sir Staples had lost the game. So the metaphor here is that everyone must play the game with wicked people, just as we do today in politics, education, and in our families. We wager our lives in the game, and some players might lose a few body parts to the evil gamblers in a chemical civilization. There is more fear in avoidance than in the actual games with the evil gambler. Choose the game, wager a hand, an ear, an eye, or more, and see what might happen in a trickster story. Most people live in fear of the game, and yet we must balance the forces of evil in the games over our ordinary lives.

In *Bearheart* the forces of evil are even greater because of the loss of gasoline at the end of a chemical civilization. Here are the most wicked games, and the most powerful postmodern metaphors of an evil gambler on the abandoned interstate highways. The world is out of balance, and we secure a sense of presence, our very survivance, in native trickster stories, and that means games with the evil gamblers. Where do we hear such stories today? Where do we witness a trickster performance that outwits evil? Whose stories could outwit such banal evil as the monarch of unleaded gasoline? Would a journalist accept the wager of a life for a few gallons of precious gasoline? Proude Cedarfair prevails and defeats the evil monarch in a traditional native dish game. The trickster Naanabozho, in one version of an *anishinaabe* creation story, plays the same dish game and defeats the evil gambler.

ARL: One other picaresque episode is the encounter at the Scapehouse on Callus Road. What lies behind that story?

GV: This was a secure house of wounded women, a postindian sanctuary in the ruins of representation. The scapehouse was a sovereign state declared by a group of very diverse women who live by a philosophy of survivance. And much of their trouble in life had been caused by men and the institutions ruled by men, or wicked traditions, so they declared a sovereign scapehouse, or a house of quiet escapes and survivance stories. With something of the instinctive sense of animals, they maintained an escape distance. The scenes at the scapehouse play on these metaphors of cultural wounds and escape distance near a reservation. The scapehouse women held the outside world at bay, and that, of course, was their greatest weakness. They lived in a garden without teases, a sanctuary removed from the games of the evil gambler. The scapehouse scenes are roads not taken, the tricky tensions of terminal creeds and survivance.

The thirteen women of the scapehouse had no need for men, and those few men who enter that weird and sensitive garden lost their erotic rights of privacy. No man had a reserved right of lust. The presence of a man in the scapehouse was communal, no more than a shared sexual practice. Benito Saint Plumero, one of the pilgrim clowns, a nickname he earned in prison, arrived at the bright orange door of the scapehouse dressed in his finest native ribbon shirt and leather trousers, one of the chosen few to enter the humid gardens. The women grew their own food, as you know, and they ate the cats, birds, and other pets that lived in the house. Likewise, men were not exclusive pets. Bigfoot was his other name, and he always said it with a tricky smile. Yes, he had big feet, and a huge penis. The invitation to the garden was obvious, and the practice was clear, but not as a private experience. Bigfoot was caught and shared by the women of the scapehouse, and they named every memorable dick that entered their garden after chief executives. Bigfoot's dick was named the President Jackson. Sister Eternal Flame, who was particularly taken by his glorious uncircumcised executive, had named other dicks after lesser presidents.

ARL: Gerald, what about the fast food fascists?

GV: My favorite fascists of the edible menus. You can see them today, everywhere, either waiting for the last gallon of gasoline or throwing trash out the window. Sir Cecil Staples is the monarch of gasoline and a fast food fascist. The fascists drive through and order fast food because they have no other sense of place, no imagined place to go, but even so, the fascists are in a great hurry to get there. Surely the most banal taste of fast food was not, at the same time, the most significant of experiences, but it seems that the ecophysiology of eating by car evolved into a new generation of fascists. The fascists drive up to the service window with a full tank of gas, always ready to drive anywhere with a burger and fries in Styrofoam containers, but with no story or place to eat. Truly, these new fascists are the anxious race, worried that one day, as they are eating fast food by car, the chemical culture that created their mobility might come to a sudden end and run out of precious gas, as it does with such violence in *Bearheart*. That particular episode about the fast food fascists is in the Witch Hunt Restaurant, located on the interstate near Ponca City, in Oklahoma. The only way to get around when the gas runs out is to walk the interstates, and that's what my native pilgrims and thousands of other people are doing in the novel. They must avoid the back roads because every turn and intersection is possessed by angry people who live in small towns. The back roads were closed to outsiders, and no one was allowed to walk through small towns. Only the interstate highways were wide and free, but not at the exits ramps, not at food stops, and certainly not in rest areas. The fast food fascists ruled parts of the interstates, and roving criminals claimed fast food restaurants as new empires of the world rising out of the ruins of a chemical civilization. These wicked empires continued the wasted vision of a great nation through the glossy menus of a fast food restaurant. The bright pictures of fast food were almost edible at the fascist restaurants. The pictures were eaten, but not yet edible.

ARL: More grave still, is it not, is the episode involving the plastic faces?

GV: Robert, that episode, "Hlastic Haces and Scolioma Moths," is the horror, the horror of *Bearheart*. Near Dumfries, Iowa, the horror, the horror, as the pilgrims encounter hundreds of deformed and crippled people on the road. The rivers are dead zones, birds crash out of the sky, fish are poisoned, and many people on the road have lost body parts to various cancers. There were children without smiles, wildly disfigured by cancers, who wore plastic faces, and who could not close their lips on the words "plastic faces," and so they said, "hlastic haces." The muscles, bone, and teeth were visible beneath the plastic masks, and they spoke in a very peculiar way. The chemicals are always there, beneath the masks of civilization, and now we must wait on the stories of plastic faces, the cancerous hlastic haces.

Little Big Mouse, the innocent, beautiful blonde in the novel, danced on the road with the cripples. She was too ecstatic to see the horror, the horror, and so she teased an old woman, "What happened to your arms?" The old woman answered, "Lost them in a rain storm," the poison rain. Pure Gumption and the mongrels were natural healers on the road; they could sense the phantom limbs of the cripples. Bigfoot said, "Cripples are part animal," and they were mighty animals. The second horror in that episode is that the young blonde, generous, and bearing none of the faults of a selfish person, recognized the excitement of disabilities, and yet how sad it was that so many people were incomplete, disfigured by chemical poisons. Little Big Mouse was beautifully complete among cripples, and that creates another horror of this scene in *Bearheart*, the cruel tension of physical differences, the celebration of physical beauty over the cancerous, twisted, and eroded bodies.

Little Big Mouse was touched by a fantastic procession of scolioma moths. They wore sensational compound eye masks and flopped their wide polyphemus wings down the road, and the blonde ran along with the smallest moths. She told the moths that she was once a moth in a dream and flew into the night with the stars. She asked one of the moths on the road if she could wear his wings. The scolioma moths turned over their wings in silence, and then they attacked the blonde because she was so perfect. Finally, the plastic faces returned to the road. Little Big Mouse said, "Parts of bodies do not make the person whole," and those were the words of her demise. She was carried away by the cripples and torn into parts. She had aroused those who were missing parts, and they wanted to devour the blonde, to magically consume parts of her body into their own. The moths and plastic faces were in a state of absolute ecstasy, and they completely devoured Little Big Mouse. They pulled her limbs off, tore her fingers out, removed every part and bone of her body and ate everything, even her blond hair, as they danced on the road to their demise.

ARL: Another episode involves a lovely invention, the word hospital. What lies behind your creation of that federal institution?

GV: Really, no fiction there but the emergency care. Native words are in bad health, natural metaphors have been weakened by the social sciences, and many native trickster stories suffer from malnutrition, and the federal government created word hospitals. The Bioavaricious Regional Word Hospitals, in *Bearheart*, were established to study the breakdown of traditional families, law and order, and the desecration of institutions as the obvious failure of language. So the government funded nine regional word hospitals in the country. The pilgrims visited one hospital that studied words with a dianoetic chromatic encoder. The doctors strained to explain that every word in the language has been color coded, and the values of the colors are studied in the possessive pronouns and tricky verbs in texts by Dennis Banks, Patricia Hearst, and Charles Manson. Richard Nixon's transcripts should have been studied by the word doctors, but for some obscure reason his conspiracies were never considered. Naturally, and in the best tradition of the social sciences, the word doctors were not able to reach any conclusions about language.

The federal government has funded an enormous amount of research that amounts to about the same thing as the study of color coded words at a regional word hospital. My novel only embellishes the interest of the federal government in studies of our ordinary use of language. For instance, the critical debate over federal funds for multicultural education suggests that the government might support studies of word wars and the politics of language. *Bearheart* carries this debate to an obvious conclusion, the actual creation of regional word hospitals to study the causes of the protracted word wars in the nation. Over the years there have been many fatalities at the hands of verbal terrorists, and millions of ordinary citizens have been wounded by pronoun insurgencies. So the word hospitals were dedicated to the study of the violence and sickness in language as the primary cause of the word wars. Conservatives argued that if we could just return to the original, foundational values of a family language and come back to the traditional ways once spoken with ease on street corners, our nation could once again be great. The problem, you see, is that the simulations of families were exposed. But again, there is nothing very fictional about the word wars, as the government has already supported film ratings and other measures of words. Listen, the universities have taken up politically correct speech with a vengeance. Clearly, the government has supported far more bizarre research in the social sciences than the Bioavaricious Regional Word Hospitals.

ARL: These episodes give the novel its flavor, its texture, its momentum. As they head toward Chaco Canyon, what have the pilgrims learned en route?

GV: Much to do about violence, and most of my native pilgrims have not lost their sense of motion as the primary reality of sovereignty. One by one natives either learned how to play a new game of survivance or lose to the evil gamblers on the road to

Chaco Canyon in New Mexico. The pilgrims who died on the journey lost the games because of their own greed, intensities, cultural reductions, traditional simulations, terminal creeds, absolutist views, and because of their temptations to court authority. Belladonna Darwin Winter Catcher, for instance, was invited with the other pilgrims to join a community of famous hunters and bucking horse breeders who lived behind the Great Wall of Orion in Oklahoma. Once inside, the hunters and breeders were courteous as they entertained the pilgrims over dinner, but little did the pilgrims know that terminal creeds were a signature of death. Belladonna was introduced as the after-dinner speaker by a very serious banker breeder, and she was so taken with *indian* simulations that she missed the cues of her own demise. She announced that she was an *indian* of traditions and would never be white. The hosts wondered about her use of the word *indian*, and she was defensive, posing in a simulation that *indians* lived closer to nature and Mother Earth. First the hunters and breeders teased her sense of *indian* blood and sacred traditions, and then, as she took cover in narcissistic terminal creeds, the hosts suddenly praised her simulations and served her a poison sugar cookie. The poison cookie was dessert for narcissists who stood by their terminal creeds. Belladonna ate the cookie and died on the road, a perfect simulation of victimry.

ARL: What's a panic hole, one of your frequent references?

GV: Panic is creation, and the hole is a trickster story. Shout into a panic hole and listen to creation, shout at the earth and the seasons change. Panic is natural, and the shout is survivance. The earth, plants, birds, and animals love to hear our shouts, and we are much wiser for the sound of our game. Shout, shout into panic holes, and the earth restores the balance.

ARL: What does it signify to have visited the fourth world?

GV: Robert, my response must be evasive. The fourth world is a native metaphor, a trace of the unnameable, an originary story. The fourth world is tacit motion and a mythic sense of sovereignty. I must be evasive in this way, only to tease motion and that sense of violence in trickster creation stories. That sense of motion in the fourth world, or transmotion, is native survivance in *Bearheart*, and the violence of mythic transmutation is not moralistic and is never mere victimry. I mean that creation stories in other cultures disguise violence, and the mythic tease of transmutation, or say visionary resurrection, is storied only after suffering, sacrifice, or victimry. Some readers are served consumer morals and want forever a trickier creation story.

ARL: What, then, were the early responses to your novel?

GV: When *Bearheart* was first published, a friend of mine assigned the novel in her class at a community college in Minneapolis. She trusted me as a writer, as a former journalist for the *Minneapolis Tribune*, and was certain the students would like my work. She read native literature as a representation of culture and taught her students to do the same. So the students were shocked to read tricky violence and native transformations in *Bearheart*. My friend called me and insisted that I visit her class the next day to explain my novel, a way to save face with her students. My novel had been published only a few weeks earlier, and that morning, in her literature class, was my first public discussion of my interpretations of *Bearheart*. The students did not expect me to tease the subject of violence and evil gamblers. My stories of the novel, and about literature in general, were mythic stories of transformation and survivance, and not a course on naturalism or realism.

I walked down the hall and could actually feel the heat coming out of the classroom. They were angry about *Bearheart*. There were about fifty students, more women than men, and older than the average students in college. They had returned to finish their degrees, and their myths were much closer to cultural representations than native transformations. They were very angry about the violence in *Bearheart*. Specifically, the students were angry about the descriptive violence toward native women in the novel. My first response was to say, "What, then, is not true in this novel?" The students could not think of anything untrue in *Bearheart*. So the descriptive scenes of violence were what troubled them, not that the scenes were not true. The students agreed to that much and seemed to recognize the irony of their anger. I then said, "What scenes in this novel have you not already read in your daily newspaper?" Listen, that question alone took the heat out of the moment, and as the students considered the two sources, they realized, in fact, that they had already read about far more horrible things going on in the world in ordinary newspaper reports than were created in my novel. Then we got down to what gave this encounter its most significant meaning. Compared to newspaper stories, there was something more haunting and troubling in the creation of my characters, the metaphors, and the scenes in *Bearheart*. I teased the construction of the moment and said, "If you think *Bearheart* is difficult to read, then imagine how haunting it was for me to write."

ARL: Do you mean that you were haunted by your own novel?

GV: Yes, many scenes in *Bearheart* are haunting, no doubt about that, and for that reason, many scenes, unlike journalism, were dangerous to create in a story. The ironies of innocence and violence, love and greed, as in the scenes with Little Big Mouse, scolioma moths, and hlastic haces, are the scenes that haunted me the most in the novel. Literature should be haunting, and at least troubling, no less than the ironies of experience. The stories in *Bearheart* arise from extraordinary visionary experiences, something of the dangers of a shamanic journey. I mean by danger that a visionary might not return to the ordinary from such extreme journeys. Many scenes in the novel are dangerous in that way, although I wasn't conscious of it at the time. I would go out for a walk late at night, after writing for most of the day, and struggle with the immediate memories of the stories. I rented a small office in downtown Saint Paul to work on *Bearheart*. I was comfortable and productive in the ordinary sense of the working world, and was more relaxed eating my lunch with others in a crowded and rushed restaurant in the building. That's not always the case, but at the time, and working on such haunting stories, that was a safe environment. I would start early in the morning on revisions of the writing done the day before, stop for lunch, and then try to finish at least a rough draft of another chapter, or say ten to fifteen new pages, in the afternoon. I wrote first on yellow legal pads to start a scene and then used a manual typewriter to finish the first rough draft. I wrote, for instance, a rough draft of scenes in the Witch Hunt Restaurant after lunch, and then reviewed that early the next morning in my office. I then turned to my notes made the night before and started the scenes in a new chapter, such as "Westward on Witching Sticks."

ARL: Where were you living then?

GV: I was living alone then, and usually ate alone in family restaurants. Several times a week, however, I joined friends for dinner, and then, more often than not, returned to work, to write at least outline notes of scenes in a new chapter. Obviously, this was very concentrated and high-energy work. I could not easily sleep at the end of the day. My mind was so active with my characters that ordinary conversations hardly distracted me from traces of scenes in the novel. I would go out for a walk late at night to change my concentration, to search for visual distractions. The walks, however, were spiritually dangerous. I lived in terror, as if, in fact, the characters of my creation were on the streets. Many of the horrible scenes in the novel were about me, and with me on the streets, and the characters almost made me an aesthetic victim of my own stories. I worried about the signs of being a victim, about any encounters on the street so late at night. I had rented a suite of rooms in a mansion on Summit Avenue in Saint Paul. I wrote dangerous scenes of a novel by day, and then was worried about my stories at night. I had created a terrible fear of violence in my own life. I was not prepared to play games with an evil gambler late at night on the streets.

So something had to change to outwit the temptations of victimry. The problem, it seemed to me then, was that I was playing the unintended role of a victim, and ironically, that was exactly what my novel was confronting, the cruel games of victimry. My new game was to simulate the perpetrator rather than the victim late at night. I created an aesthetic simulation of the perpetrator and teased that haunting connection to the victim. I walked the streets as a literary perpetrator. I was fearless in narrow, dark alleys, and even paused on the most dangerous corners in Saint Paul. I posed as a menace in a game with the evil gamblers on the streets. My pose, however, soon ended with an even greater concern over my public appearance. I could have been the perfect suspect if a crime had occurred in the course of my poses as a perpetrator. My responses to the police would have been preposterous. You see, officer, my literary game is shamanic, an act of survivance, and very dangerous. Tonight, you see, my pose is the simulation of a perpetrator to outwit the evil gambler in my stories of victimry. My rights to remain silent were not aesthetic. I decided on a wiser course of action and more ironic manner of a worried writer at the bar in the Commodore Hotel in Saint Paul. There, late at night, other writers seemed to be worried about their own evil gamblers.

7

Griever in China

ARL: In your second novel, *Griever: An American Monkey King in China*, the style of carnivalesque, of picturesque, of journey, is still very present. All, in a way, is located inside that title figure's name, Griever de Hocus. Who is this character?

GV: Griever is a loose storier, my eternal holosexual trickster, a native mind monkey. The trickster is a presence, not an absence, and the sure motion of native sovereignty. He appears in several of my earlier stories, but this is his first novel, a memorable pose as a tricky teacher in the People's Republic of China. Once, when he liberated rather than dissected frogs in a science class, and croaked around the room, the teacher named him King of the Frogs. That gesture of sovereignty was his best start in trickster stories. Griever, as you know, is memorable for three curious gestures, his tricky meditative moves, but he is not a serious griever like his mother. He leans back and taps the toes of his shoes together, pinches and folds his ear, and forever turns a single strand of hair on his right temple. The toe taps are moments of delight, something of an applause. The meaning of these gestures is obscure, but they are his signatures in the novel.

Coffee, his mother, was always taken with signatures. That's how she remembers people, by their curious gestures, and she named her son that way, in honor of griever meditation, a signature practice she learned from an elusive gypsy who visited the White Earth Reservation. He was a member of a caravan named the Universal Hocus Crown. Coffee learned in the hocus of their passion play that griever meditation cured headaches and the common cold, and many other problems. She was a convert to griever time, convinced that she could restore a sense of spiritual balance, as one does in serious meditation, by grieving on a regular schedule, and so she became the first traditional native griever on the reservation. Griever, in fact, was conceived during griever meditation, and then the caravan was gone overnight.

ARL: Griever is from the White Earth Reservation, but the novel also arises out of the semester you spent teaching at Tianjin University. Did you need to go to China to write this book?

GV: Maybe, but at the time I had no plans to write anything about China. Laura, my wife, and I had accepted invitations to teach literature and English at Tianjin University. We had planned to stay for the academic year, but near the end of the first semester my mother was hospitalized, so we returned to California. I had considered writing an essay or editorial article on my experiences, but in the end decided against the idea because of the cultural contradictions. The limitations were obvious, and my brief experience in such a complex culture was not enough to write about at the time. However, my view changed when we were taken to a performance of the Monkey King, episodic scenes of the opera *Havoc of Heaven*. The children were very excited, and families rushed to the stage when their favorite scenes were performed. The Monkey King was a distinct measure of cultural pleasure. The audience was exuberant, and people talked and changed seats several times during the performance, and at the end there was no applause. That very active, dynamic audience, however, was not what inspired me to consider a novel about my experiences in China.

ARL: Trickster transformations?

GV: I was taken with the obvious, as if the trickster was on his first date. The Chinese Monkey King, or Mind Monkey, was a transformational character related to Naanabozho, the *anishinaabe* trickster. Clearly, these two wonderful trickster characters are cousins, and that coincidence of transmotion was the start of my novel. I decided then to bring these two fantastic characters together in name, creation, irony, cultural play, and cousinry. I wrote notes there, and later, on my return, constructed scenes that would become a novel. Everything changed, of course, as the trickster carried out some of my experiences and fantasies of political confrontations. I was a visiting professor at Tianjin University. Griever, in the novel, is a teacher at Zhou Enlai University in Tianjin. He travels with a wise rooster and subverts the government, outwits corrupt authorities, and tricks some of the same administrators on my wish list at the university.

ARL: Transformation might almost be the name of the entire textual game in the novel. Not only Griever himself but the rooster who keeps him company. Who is this rooster?

GV: Matteo Ricci is the rooster of deliverance, and the tricky chicken of native survivance. Griever liberated the great cock at the street market and ordained him then and there with a new name. Griever, in fact, could not stand to watch the cutthroat bleed the birds, so he bought the freedom of every caged chicken at the market. Matteo Ricci is a prancer, and the trickster holds his bright cock on a tether. Griever was known as a comic liberator and a riotous, subversive teacher, and that tricky persona was understood and tolerated in the context of the many stories and opera scenes of the Chinese Monkey King in *The Journey to the West*.

ARL: Griever has no hesitation in freeing these birds, any birds. You could almost say he became not only the Monkey King but the Chicken King?

GV: Griever is the mighty king of frogs, chickens, and many creatures, and once he ransomed the caged birds. Others at the market shouted out that he must free the garlic, free the melons, free the cabbage, and you name the vegetables waiting to be liberated for a price. The chickens scurried out of sight of the cutthroat once they were free, but by the end of the day most of the cocks and hens fluttered back to their cages in the market. Caged birds turned lonesome on the run, and the cultural allegories were obvious in the People's Republic of China.

ARL: Is that why, throughout the novel and indeed at its ending, you associate the trickster so strongly with avian images, images of flight?

GV: Griever is always in tricky motion, and the totemic image of flight is native survivance. Crows, eagles, chickens, and other birds are present in most of my stories, along with many tricky mongrels. More to the point, my ancestors are of the *anishinaabe* crane totem, and my turns and stories of creation are more avian than arboreal, contrary to my tease of bears at the treelines. Matteo Ricci is an avian tracer and a wise presence in bright feathers. He is by name a historical voice in the narrative, a contentious pose that teases the obvious as he rides with me and the trickster. That Cochin China cock with the name of a cultural adventurer is an ironic turn of obvious political and historical situations.

There are many trickster voices in my stories, as ironies and narrative teases of history. Matteo Ricci is a mighty teaser with great feathered legs. Griever, at the end of the novel, takes flight in an ultralight airplane. Matteo Ricci, always at his side, soars with the trickster to Macao.

ARL: And yet the texture of much of the novel is extremely earth-bound. There is a great deal of earth, blood, excrement, sexuality, throughout this book. I assume a contrast you wanted to draw is between being both above and of the earth?

GV: Perhaps the rat hunter and the chapter about the tricky pigs on the island are good examples. Sandie, the rat hunter, shot rodents on the run near the canals, on the street, on the campus, anywhere. He had a license to kill, and tied the many dead rats to his belt. *Lao shu, lao shu*, the hunter shouted on the streets, rats, rats. The hunt, however, was much more than a slow method of extermination. Many people ate rat meat, the thin flank and what little they could nibble off the bones, and used the hides to make shoes for children. Sandie, it turned out, was a tricky survivor of the cultural revolution, a rat hunter with a doctorate in political science and economics from the University of California.

Griever, in the chapter "Obo Island," plays basketball with domestic pigs. The sows nose the ball down the court to the boars. The names of the pigs are painted in bold characters on their sides. The trickster was told that one pig was named Horse, another Ant, and another China Red. Obo Island was a sanctuary for wise pigs, warriors, clowns, and tricksters. Griever teased the stone shaman, the moth walker, the mute pigeon, and the great healers and dealers on the island that was a reservation.

Griever is a holosexual trickster, an erotic perpetrator of many genders. Sugar Dee, a blond lesbian teacher, was taken with the trickster at the market. She was aroused by his many gestures, by his liberative manner at the market, and by his sovereign way with the chickens. Sugar Dee wore a print dress with two large poppies that flowered over her breasts. Griever runs his hands under the bright flowers and in the rush becomes a woman in an erotic market scene. She, he, "towed her flesh back from the cold and heard the cocks and animals on her breath." Later in the novel the trickster sexes a student translator at a pavilion near the beach. They lust in the scent of garlic. Matteo Ricci bounces on the rail, out of breath with the lovers.

ARL: Gerald, who is Hester Hua Dan?

GV: The Chinese classical opera creates four main roles for actors: the *sheng*, or male roles; the *jing*, or painted faces; the *chou*, or clowns; and the *dan*, or female roles. The *dan* actors were once men. Colin Mackerras writes in *The Performing Arts in Contemporary China* that the male *dan* was part of a feudal society that is not courted today. So there are five roles of the *dan*: the proper matron; the comic or mischievous role; the warrior; the older, mature woman; and *hua dan*, the ever-charming, vivacious woman of amorous gestures.

Hester Hua Dan is a translator and the daughter of Egas Zhang, the sinister chain smoker and foreign affairs director at Tianjin University. Griever, at first notice, was charmed by the young, innocent translator. He touched her by chance of motion on a crowded bus and was aroused by her gestures, the twitch of a muscle at the corner of her mouth, a moist scar on her cheek, and a signature jade rabbit on a chain around her neck. He would be haunted forever by that necklace. Griever was a much wiser trickster for the innocence of that translator. Hester was amorous and vivacious but not as seductive as the *hua dan* actors in the opera. Later, when she told him she was pregnant, the trickster was ecstatic, but her father hated foreigners and ordered her to have an abortion.

Egas Zhang could not bear another foreign devil in his family. His wife gave birth to a blond daughter while he was away as a translator in Africa. Battle Wilson, a Sinophile and petroleum engineer, was the father, and he died in the earthquake at Tangshan. The blond child was named Kangmei. Egas took advantage of his disgrace to abuse foreign teachers and his family. Griever, wise to his wicked smile, prepared for an early departure on an ultralight airplane to Macao. Kangmei, a mysterious creation who wears a burnoose and raises silkworms, was eager to leave the country. Hester, however, resisted the idea of an avian escape because she was determined to have an abortion. Griever might have convinced his *hua dan* to be an actor in other operas, but the trickster never had the chance. Hester and Kuan Yin, their unborn daughter with the same name as the bodhisattva, were drowned by Egas Zhang. Later that night their bodies were found in a blue light at the murky bottom of the fish pond on campus. The jade rabbit necklace was tied around her neck.

ARL: In all of this ventriloquy you take aim at not only colonial malpractice but also Chinese malpractice, and especially authoritarianism. Monkey and trickster are ways of subverting that, the double thrusts to this story?

GV: Subversion was the reality of teaching there, as it is everywhere, but the risks are greater in the People's Republic of China. Your notice of the "double thrust" is doubled in both name and practice. The Communist Party established a shadow authority over the usual administrators of academic departments at Tianjin University. The shadow players carried out the material means of power rather than the curious authority of academic discourse, and that, of course, invited the best of sycophancy, corruption, subversion, and the end of irony. So buried were the stories, the contradictions of the revolution, as you know, that mere manners and slapstick were comic treats. The shadow cadre acted with such fealty, mock generosity, and puny courtesy on campus that their entire show was ironic. Dangerous, to be sure, and always ironic. The slightest comic nudge cracked the tedious power plays, and trickster stories were the most subversive, it seemed to me at the time. Obviously, the chances of irony were not always present, but in my novel the shadow cadre lost their clothes.

Griever, in my tricky interests, changed the music that was broadcast over the loudspeakers one early morning on the campus. He replaced the glorious and patriotic recording of "The East Is Red" with "The Stars and Stripes Forever" by John Philip Sousa. Matteo Ricci marched to the new music, and the sound of those sweet piccolos summoned many men in uniform to investigate the subversion. I waited for the chance and then turned to trickster stories.

ARL: And your stories have always been ironic and aimed to subvert?

GV: The Communist cadre are *indian* agents, and that is a critical irony. Listen, if native survivance is natural reason, then the shadow cadre practiced fealty reason at Tianjin University. The clichés of the cultural revolution set a natural edge of irony and, at the same time, the humdrum poses of uniformed men created an unnatural state of absolute conformity. Such mundane cues are an absence, much like the absence of natives in the simulations of the *indian*, and this revolutionary absence is played against a great national literature, a literature of extraordinary imagination, tricky wisdom, and cultural subtleties. Could this be a timeless literature? No, not really, that idea is way beyond the reach of the shadow cadre. Maybe the stories that endure are tricky performances that have always been part of this great nation, a culture of transformations and family play, much greater than revolutions. The Monkey King, of course, plays against these newcomers with their ideologies of absolute control, with their skeptical surges of denial, the material denial of irony, mystery, and always the revisions of history.

The Monkey King performances were apparently never revised, and the popular comic operas were produced onstage even at the nasty heart of the revolution. Colin Mackerras points out that traditional opera was revived, in part, because it was revolutionary and created a sense of "active optimism." Yet the terminal creeds of a material revolution missed the ironies of a tricky creation story. The *anishinaabe* oral stories of Naanabozho, however, were revised in translation by missionaries and others, and once published, those revisions became the dominant versions of the stories. So the monkey and trickster characters are comparable, but the revisions of the stories are not because of cultural translations. The Communist Chinese converted many other stories to serve the revolution, such as the stories about wicked landlords and evil capitalists. Comparable, no doubt, but for different reasons, the missionaries revised native trickster stories with monotheistic morals.

ARL: The Monkey King was already an allegory of transformation, if not cultural revolution. Is that an accurate interpretation?

GV: The Monkey King and the trickster Naanabozho are both cultural allegories and transformations that are not easily revised to serve the real, or representations of political authority. Even so, any cultural revisions would demand an extraordinary sense of literary irony, and that, in itself, would be a very tricky story. Trickster stories, in fact, have a built-in destruct metaphor that overturns the obvious, and trying to change that would be like trying to represent the pieties of governance in a political cartoon. There are differences, of course, in the way these cultural stories have been presented, which is not the same as cultural revisions. I mean, for one thing, the monkey is heard in stories and seen in operas, and the written language of the performance is the same as the original stories. Now, the trickster Naanabozho was seen in the oral stories of the *anishinaabe*, and then the stories were translated into various written languages. The translation or presentation of these stories in other languages was a cultural revision, but the storiers and the tricksters are artists of transmutation, and the cultural allegories of the stories are in the metaphors of native motion, or the transmotion of survivance.

The Naanabozho stories were oral performances, but before natives could put their stories to writing, they suffered the indignities of discovery, monotheistic piety, and colonial dominance. The pleasurable stories of the trickster were taken over by social scientists and presented as cultural evidence. In other words, the translations of Naanabozho stories are simulations. Monkey and trickster are related by creation, the natural cousins of cultural ironies, as if these tricky characters were the very allegories of survivance, and the universal stories of transmutation that would forever outwit evil gamblers and authoritarian cultures. Griever de Hocus, then, in this sense of trickster cousinry, is the American Monkey King in China.

ARL: Griever constantly, in another phrase of yours, loosens the seams of culture. Is that what lies behind the freeing of the chickens?

GV: Buddhist monks once prayed and meditated over more than a million chickens terminated by the government in Hong Kong. Griever, as a chicken liberator, was there with the monks in spirit, but the gassing and slashing of chickens at the time would not have been a good story for the trickster because it was carried out to control the possible spread of avian influenza. Griever frees chickens, as he did at the market, but not sick chickens. He would have meditated with monks and then loosened the seams of natural immunities to save the chickens, and that, in a trickster story, would have been an act of native reason and survivance. Griever, you see, liberates antibodies and chickens.

Griever has a tricky brilliance, and his performances truly liberate people in stories. I gave him my notes, my comments, and some of my everyday experiences at Tianjin University. However, as you know, the novel did not take shape for at least a year after my return. Naturally, my experiences had to be believable as a trickster story on the page, and so that explains my use of cultural and historical references. Here, the seams were loosened, but not too much, because the trickster moves more wisely in the context of culture, and historical events are easier to overturn and show a native act of liberation and survivance. These are not oral trickster stories, and so the performance must be created in some obvious tease of culture and history. There are, as you know, more historical references in this novel than in my other stories, and that because of the many tricky poses and performances.

Griever loosened the seams of my own experiences as a teacher, and he could do that in the context of the Monkey King. The trickster took advice from the gatekeeper at the university. Wu Chou, the warrior clown, was an actor in the opera *Havoc of Heaven* and earned his name from the classical theater. Griever, he said, was a holosexual clown, and so he painted the trickster's face in the tradition of the theater. My novel owes much to the thoughts of other writers. For instance, Simon Leys, in *Chinese Shadows*, wrote that the "way in which daily speech was filled with expressions and metaphors taken from the stage clearly attested to the hold that theater had over life." The Monkey King, you see, could be storied and seen on the streets, and the trickster could be seen as an actor in the context of the theater. That the trickster is a teacher is twice the act and cultural irony. Griever was a trickster in a popular comic opera as a foreign teacher. He was a *hua lian* actor, a painted face, and a *wu chou*, or warrior clown, and his tricky actions were in the cause of truth and liberation. My characters, in this sense, are created in the intellectual tradition of the freedom of thought, and the stories of transformation could be an inspiration to those readers who might loosen the seams of authoritarian governments.

ARL: What's China Browne's role in the novel?

GV: Griever writes several letters to China Browne. Two of these letters are the start and close of the novel. He writes about his arrival and dreams on his first night in the country. Matteo Ricci and Kangmei are mentioned in the last letter, and he describes their avian adventure on an ultralight airplane over the mountains and vast countryside to Macao. China's brother,

Slyboots Browne, actually built the ultralight airplane. Griever, China, and her brother are from the White Earth Reservation in Minnesota. China arrived, in the first chapter of the novel, at Tianjin University. She was there to interview Wu Chou about Griever, her cousin by native adoption, and to continue her research on Alicia Little and the Natural Foot Society in China.

China Browne comes from a family of tricksters on the reservation. She pretended, as a child, that her feet were bound, golden lotuses under blue bandannas, and so she earned the name China. She is a character in my novel *The Trickster of Liberty*, and she is mentioned in *Hotline Healers: An Almost Browne Novel*. Griever was convinced that once the Chinese soared in the Patronia Microlights built by Slyboots they would buy millions of them and transform the country. The trickster of avian visions thought the people would rather have an ultralight airplane than an automobile. Griever was wrong about that, but he was right to escape on an ultralight to Macao.

ARL: Hester Hua Dan was trained as a translator in the novel, and, in a way, is your literary rationale one of translation?

GV: George Steiner writes that translation is an act of love that starts with trust, but when it fails because of "blurred perception," translation traduces. Robert, to answer your question in this context, much of what has been translated by social scientists about natives has traduced, because of a failure of trust and perception. Traduced the creative energy of oral stories and the tricky sense of chance and native reason. Chinese literature, however, was translated as artistic creation and not traduced by social scientists. The Monkey King stories were translated as a creative act of love by Anthony C. Yu in *The Journey to the West*, and by Arthur Waley in *Monkey*. Our conversation about this would be much different today if native stories had been translated by artists who loved native stories, rather than by men who traduced native creation. My novel is a translation, in a sense, of trickster teases, an act of love and survivance. These mighty tricksters come together in the book, in the same stories, and we are better for their literary cousinry.

ARL: And *Griever* overall, is that, too, in and of itself, another kind of performance, the textual maneuvers, inversions, and the culture play?

GV: Yes, literary performance is at the very heart of my stories and novels. I could not easily come to this creative performance by character, by trickster motion, or by descriptive scenes, as a teacher on a mere literary adventure. *Griever* is my second novel, one of my best performances and translations of trickster survivance stories. I am now the writer and the reader, twice the translator of my own stories. I start the act of trust and love in these stories of tricksters. My trickster characters must overturn the politics of nations in stories, as nations must traduce the best creations of literature.

ARL: Many of your novels have extensive bibliographies. Why so?

GV: Clearly, the research, ideas, and stories by many authors are very important to me, especially in preparation to write *Griever*. I also read many studies and histories of Christopher Columbus in the creation of my novel *The Heirs of Columbus*. I read many books and articles to write these two novels, and made extensive notes about historical situations, political contradictions, and cultural anecdotes. I worked much of that material into various scenes in the novels. Most place-names are based on historical documents. I found an old map, for instance, that recorded the many colonial concessions in Tianjin. I used these earlier street names and other references in my novel and doubled the history. Griever noted the street names in various concession districts, such as Saint Louis Boulevard, Gaston Kahn, Elgin Road, London Meadows, Matsushima Road, and Victoria Park. Chinese literary, political, and historical figures are present in my stories. Many of my characters are avian, and they fly so far out of ordinary sight in the book that historical connections are important to give some comfort to the reader. I either mention sources in the actual narrative or provide bibliographic information at the end of the novels. Some editors have resisted my practice of noting sources and argued that citations in fiction may distract the reader. Maybe, but my sources are part of my work. I could just as well not mention my preparation of the novel, but I feel a duty to the reader to show my sources, my traces of inspiration, and the good thoughts of many scholars. Recently, for instance, I studied the history of the Holy Rule of Saint Benedict to write a story about the *Manabozho Curiosa*, a monastic manuscript, in my novel *Hotline Healers*. I listed most of my sources in the narrative, such as *The Montecassino Passion* by Robert Edwards.

ARL: John Updike, in his novel *Bech*, once included a fictional bibliography. You must have had the same temptation to create sources in your novels.

GV: Yes, of course, but why would an author create bibliographic sources only to disguise the actual sources? There are no convincing reasons to do that in my novels. I must establish and then tease historical realities in the interests of my tricky characters, who overturn the obvious. Yet novelists create everything, the characters, the authors, titles, and scenes as history. The *Manabozho Curiosa* is my creation of a native monastic manuscript, for instance, but the notice and ironic sense of this title is rather obvious in the narrative. The only way some readers can be sure is to check out the sources in a library.

8

Tricksters of Liberty

ARL: Gerald, is your third novel, *The Trickster of Liberty: Tribal Heirs to a Wild Baronage*, a collection of campus stories?

GV: Maybe, but *The Trickster of Liberty* is rather an anticampus novel, you know, an academic aversion, because the trickster characters in my *liberty* stories create and reveal the consumer contradictions of institutional education. My tricky characters must buck the pretentious promises of the academy. The campus may be a sanctuary, but the tease of my stories is more than an academic station of the cross. Maybe the campus is an academic ecotone, the tensions, tones, and historical contradictions of natives in the very classrooms of cultural dominance. So natives, in this sense, are there, on the campus, but there to tease the situations of abuse and absence at an escape distance. Natives, obviously, are not on the campus by the want of history. Natives are the absence, not the presence, at universities, and that absence is the very tension of my stories, the chance and contradictions that invite tricksters to matriculate.

ARL: Yes, but could there be a trickster university?

GV: Consider the possibility that students, like trickster characters, come to the campus not just for the degrees that might enhance their income and disguises in the community, but imagine that they come because they hope to hear in four years at least one *last* lecture, you know, the last crease of tragic wisdom in a lecture. Someone who would speak about how they got to their ideas, rather than how their ideas are represented as some treasure of authority, but the mute lectures continue in many courses. Trickster characters, of course, come alive in the acid rain of academic lectures. The native trickster teases the ownership of ideas and history, that long history of territorial dominance, and the reduction of imagination to serve the causes of cultural discovery and possession. Imagine a university that encouraged the faculty to give last lectures, the synchronous creation of ideas, as if every lecture was the last one. Now, that would be almost a trickster university.

ARL: Could there be a trickster anthropology?

GV: Suppose that anthropology departments awakened to the *teases* of culture, rather than the *causes* of culture, and offered year-long seminars of *last* lectures, where the faculty gave last lectures about why they decided to study cultures in the first place. And was there anything of a tease, was there a possible relationship between a real person and experiences that might have escaped the methods of the social sciences? Now, that might be a really interesting course. Might even attract students to a new course of study in trickster hermeneutics.

ARL: The work that probably more than any other could be called antireductionist is the novel that followed *Trickster of Liberty*, namely, *The Heirs of Columbus*. Why make Christopher Columbus a Mayan?

GV: The Bering Strait migration myth or story has always fascinated me by its arrogance, that natives came here from somewhere else and did so across the Bering Strait. That tidy bit of cultural arrogance denies the origin myths of natives, the traditional myths that natives emerged from the earth here, and with a very creative understanding of their own presence. Consider the mighty migration story of N. Scott Momaday's grandmother in *The Way to Rainy Mountain*. There's no evidence that the Bering Strait migration took place in one direction or another. In fact, there may be some recent evidence suggesting that the migration took place the other way. That is, from here to there, or wherever.

So my thoughts turned to the arrogance of culture and civilization, and the migrations from Europe and the Mediterranean. The centers of civilization are not originary and exclusive but are everywhere on the earth. And there is every reason to believe that natives migrated around the world, as they once established extensive trade routes. That ethereal grant of dominion over animals and continents is a monotheistic creation story that has, at last, been shelved with so many other curios of human misadventure. Christopher Columbus was not the only traveler who had the enthusiasm and maybe stupidity to set sail in search of another continent. Natives, in fact, found him centuries earlier. My idea, you see, is that natives probably landed generations earlier in Europe and the Mediterranean. Natives, in fact, might have taught people everywhere how to build pyramids, how to do all sorts of things. There were hundreds of books and trade documents by natives that would prove their influence at the time, but unfortunately that evidence burned with the Library of Alexandria on the Mediterranean Sea. Sacred texts of the natives were lost in that fire. The barbarians burned the oceanic histories of natives in a great and universal library. The arrogance of monotheistic civilization came out of that destruction, and that arrogance continues to burden natives in their own standpoints and stories. Columbus, then, was a crossblood, a descendant of the ancient natives, and he was teased by this inheritance to return to his ancestral homeland. The irony is that he came home by mistake. I turn these histories around, of course, the encounters and events, to favor the good humor and trickery of natives. Columbus, in fact, is healed and given a much wiser presence in my tricky native stories.

The Admiral of the Ocean Sea was careless and awkward and unimaginative, and through meditation and constant attention, native shamans restored him to be a much more interesting and reasonable person than he otherwise would have become. And so that was the start of it. Then his heirs, his extended family through all these generations, have an annual storytelling event at the headwaters of the Mississippi River in Minnesota. The heirs of Columbus gather every autumn to tell their best stories about this great migration. And this is the native story of creating a tricky new nation. The native heirs, in his name, create a new nation that is dedicated to healing those who have been poisoned and wounded by the first five centuries of a monotheistic chemical civilization.

ARL: Stone Columbus, a latter-day reincarnation – who is he?

GV: Christopher Columbus is much wiser as a native in the tease of my stories than he ever was in his own time. He landed and then worried about his royal tithe, a rather common and whiny pose. "I hope to Our Lord that it will be the greatest honor for Christianity, although it has been accomplished with such ease," he wrote at the end of his journal. Yes, and with such ease his tricky heirs created the Felipa Flowers Casino at Point Assinika.

Stone Columbus could be me – well, almost, almost. That almost sounds like an overture. Stone's new nation is dedicated to heal the wounds of civilization. I would do that. Thousands of children were cured, as you know, and the cost of genetic cures was covered by the millions of dollars lost at the casino. Columbus was used by his heirs, for the first time, to create a new native nation dedicated to tricky health rather than the usual proprietary airs and rights of conquest. Actually, the wounded children were touched by new genes and healed by the light of native shamans. The shaman in me would do that, heal the wounded children with tricky stories. Everywhere the wounded wait to hear stories, to be teased, and to be healed by stories. Many of my relatives were teasers and healers with their stories. Sometimes the tease of a trickster is liberation, and no one has ever owned the tease or the stories.

ARL: The novelist as genetic engineer?

GV: Maybe, but only with a casino. Stone makes tricky use of casino cash, and it was "accomplished with such ease." Now, it seems, native casinos have overtaken my trickster stories with greed, and most of the cash goes to material simulations. Natives, at last, could change the world with casino money, but these are my stories. Natives could heal with casino money, they could even establish embassies, the natural pose of sovereignty, and negotiate with other governments to liberate stateless families. Natives could be mighty philanthropists. Casinos are a chance, a tricky chance of moral courage, but the right to heal may have been squandered once more by greedy leaders. Casinos are the end of a native romance and the last earnest tease of sovereignty.

ARL: What is the meaning of the name Point Assinika?

GV: Point Roberts, Washington, is named Point Assinika in *The Heirs of Columbus*. Point Assinika, our new tricky nation discovered five centuries to the day after Christopher Columbus returned to his homeland and the continental myth of the New World. Assinika, or *asiniikaa*, means "many stones or rocks" in the language of the *anishinaabe*, and the brother of Naanabozho the trickster is a stone. I am a stone, and stones are native stories. Stones are the presence of native stories. The firstborn in the *anishinaabe* trickster stories is a stone, and stone is envious of his brother Naanabozho because he goes everywhere and does all kinds of things. Stone has no sense of adventure but in his brother's stories. He is content, at first, to listen to stories, but he knows his brother is bothered that he cannot move. The trickster teases the stone about his permanence, about his place. So the stone decides to outwit his brother Naanabozho, and he does it with fire. "I know what you can do to get rid of me," says the stone. "I know it bothers you that you must come back and honor me as your brother, and you would rather not do this. So I want you to carefully follow my instructions so you can get rid of me forever. I want you to heat me up and then throw cold water on me." So Naanabozho does this, he heats his brother the stone in a fire, and when he pours water on him, the stone shatters into billions of pieces and covers the earth. Everywhere there are stones of that first fire of the tricksters. So no matter where you look, you can find a stone that is a trickster with a story. Stones are native stories, and stones are everywhere. I choose that name because we are stones by creation.

ARL: *The Heirs of Columbus* also offers itself as a kind of detective story. You use a number of characters in the course of a historical detection. In this connection, who is Felipa Flowers?

GV: Christopher, Stone, and Felipa are names that circle in the stories of the native heirs on the reservation. Christopher Columbus, as you know, married Dona Felipa Perestrello e Moniz in Portugal. They lived in Lisbon, and Columbus became a chartmaker and a mariner. Surely, that much was only the start of his envy.

Felipa Flowers is a native lawyer who becomes a bone trader. She would trade the bones of Christopher Columbus for the remains of Pocahontas. Felipa lives on the reservation with Stone Columbus, her daughter, Migis, and a healer mongrel with a blue tongue named Admire. Migis is named for the sacred cowrie of creation stories. The *Santa Maria Casino* was once their home, but when that burned they moved to a house trailer near the headwaters of the Mississippi River. Felipa, an heir to the ruins of native discoveries and representations, receives a letter from an antiquarian book collector who has located the remains of Pocahontas at Gravesend, England. That, of course, is a clue to one of the detective stories in the novel. So she meets him in London at a masque performance and they set out to find the bones of Lady Rebecca Rolfe, or Pocahontas, at Gravesend. Pocahontas died there, and a bronze statue honors her image in the garden of St. George's Parish. Someday there might be a statue of Felipa there too. Columbus, Pocahontas, and Felipa come together in the same stories at Gravesend.

ARL: Felipa lives again, for a time, but what is her connection to Captain Treves Brink, Chaine Riel Doumet, and Lappet Tulip Browne?

GV: You mean my family of trickster investigators? They're the kinds of investigators who can travel out of time and place, negotiate the unknown by virtual presence, and determine the mysteries that must be seen and solved in such a way as always to tell another story. Felipa, you see, is a lawyer turned trickster poacher and bone trader. She contacted a strange shaman, an urban tent shaker named Transom, to free the bones of Columbus in a vault at the Brotherhood of American Explorers in New York City. Captain Treves Brink was the investigator at the scene. This character was created by memory of a real event. Not in name, of course, but in his manner and wild red hair. The real character was a police captain in Manhattan. I was visiting the writer Stan Steiner in the late sixties, and we attended the second opening of the play *Che Guevara*. The first production was closed by the police because of nudity. Following a court hearing, the second opening was a simulation of nudity. The players wore clear plastic crotch covers stuffed with steel wool, and that production ended in the middle of the first act. A drunken police detective walked onstage, drew his revolver, and threatened to shoot the players. He seemed to be troubled by alcohol and the politics of simulated pubic hair. When the detective waved his gun, the audience ducked and rushed to the exits. The police captain was on the scene in minutes, smartly dressed, a bright investigator and tricky moderator who commanded the comedy of manners on the sidewalk in front of the theater. Simultaneously, my police captain with the red hair directed several squads of surly policemen, managed the anxious theater director, along with his assistants and angry actors, and courted a curious audience. Well, at least he courted my curiosity. Many diplomats who were there for the second production had parked their limousines with immunity in front of the theater. The limousines were blocked by police cars, and my good captain managed that at the same time too. The scene outside, you see, was much more dramatic than the actual production in the theater. So that scene came to mind in the character of Captain Treves Brink.

Doric Michéd reported that the bones of Christopher Columbus had been stolen from the Brotherhood of American Explorers. Judge Beatrice Lord, who could be a distant cousin of Miles Lord, presided over the trial in Bone Court. Captain Brink was the first witness, and he told the court that the presence of shamans was not a crime and, in fact, there was no evidence of a crime. Transom, you see, was a tent shaker, and he might not have even been in the building. There was no material evidence that a crime had actually taken place.

Chaine Riel Doumet and Lappet Tulip Browne are both natives and private investigators. They were both witnesses in Bone Court. Chaine, a retired military intelligence agent, had been hired by the federal government to investigate the casino, genetic cloning, and the heirs of Columbus. He supported the idea that tribal bones have rights and should be represented in court. Tulip was hired by the tribal government to investigate the heirs. She told stories about tricksters and made a distinction between sacred objects and the stories about bones. She said language was a game, not a rule, and so legal evidence is a story. Judge Lord never forgot her day in court with the heirs and their stories about the rights of bones. She was the first judge to allow virtual reality as evidence in court.

ARL: And what is the role of Doric Michéd in this configuration?

GV: Doric Michéd, a character who sues over a shamanic cue and a cultural tease, is not based on the manner of the late Michael Dorris, no matter the critical similarities that some readers might have contrived. However, Michéd by fiction, and Dorris by fact, were both members of explorer clubs. Sylvester Long Lance, the great poser, was also a member of the Explorers Club in New York. Michéd, Dorris, and Long Lance have that much in common, but associations of fictive explorers are not sources of native identities. Doric is bright, monied, manicured, devious, and he is a material entertainer with golden ties to civilization and dominance. This ironic character is an invitation to tricksters and shamans to tease the manners so admired by the members of the Brotherhood of American Explorers.

ARL: These "detectives" in fact seek to unravel the five centuries from Christopher Columbus to Stone Columbus. What do they discover about Pocahontas, John Smith, and John Rolfe?

GV: Felipa Flowers takes up the poses and identities of Pocahontas. She travels out of time and in other stories, as a shaman might. She travels to London, stays in the same places as the colonial princess, walks the same streets, dresses for the same masque, and in the end, recovers the bones of Pocahontas at St. George's Parish in Gravesend.

Felipa and most of my characters create a presence of natives in original histories. These stories create a native sense of transformation and survivance, a shamanic journey that may heal and liberate, but the actual outcome is a mystery. Now, many historians examine only the documents, the political and physical evidence of a cultural trial, and write out of dominance. My characters are shamanic investigators of another court. Historians continue the mistakes out of the same old continental discoveries, the absence of natives, and the crispy myths of Christopher Columbus. Felipa and the heirs, on the other hand, create a presence of natives in tricky, strategic shamanic stories of survivance. My approach is native survivance in stories, that is, to hear more than mere documents, which are already selected, already the common law, already praised to serve cultural dominance. Native stories of survivance are the creation of presence, of tricky time and place, over the absence of natives in the causal histories of civilization. Native histories are natural reason, the memories and seasons of survivance. Listen, the best stories are shamanic, and more visionary than victimry. I mentioned the visual stories of Momaday's grandmother in *The Way to Rainy Mountain*. My characters create their stories in this way. Columbus, you see, is a native story of shamanic investigations, transmutations, and many, many heirs. Columbus, in the stories of my characters, is not a season, not a demon of history. That is, he is not an eternal pose of cultural dominance. Natives are, in fact, his heirs in the tricky stories of discovery.

ARL: Another historic figure who has interested you across the years, and who makes an appearance in *The Heirs of Columbus*, is the mixedblood leader Louis Riel. What's his role in this novel?

GV: Riel was a *métis* resistance leader in Canada. Catholic, and a native visionary, he led a peaceful movement, at first, to honor the land rights of the *métis* in the face of government deceptions. Peace, however, would not be honored in the end. Canadian Mounties were beaten by the *métis* at Duck Lake, but later, at Batoche, Riel was captured, tried, and convicted of treason. He was hanged because of his resistance to the corruption of a colonial government in a native place. Riel is in our stories; he is in my novels; he is a tricky native presence in shamanic detection.

ARL: And yet another sense of presence and place is created in *The Heirs of Columbus*. Where in the novel's figuration are Genoa and Assinika?

GV: Places are created in stories, and memories of our presence in places are never easy to abandon. Genoa is a story on many maps. Assinika, a new native nation, was created in stories at a place on the map named Point Roberts, Washington. Memories may go with the stories of a native presence and with the places named on maps. Assinika is in the book, a much better place than a map. Places on this continent are native creations in the sense that the heart of stories is never an absolute history. So the creation of a native place is in the memory of the story. Places are not passive, and so the creation of a new native nation in my novel is more memorable than a mere name on the map. The place we create is the place we remember, the place we continue in stories. The *anishinaabe* creation is out of water, the presence of water as a place. We are water, and there is no presence without water and trickster stories of that creation.

9

Games of Dead Voices

ARL: What, whose, are the "dead voices" of your novel *Dead Voices?*
GV: The dead voices of social sciences, the properties of cultural studies, and the absence of natives in history. Taken seriously, the simulations of anthropology and the social sciences discount the presence of real natives, and the stories of natives are reduced in translation and by the invention of culture. The great teases of natives stories are misreckoned as an absence, and, in that sense, are *dead voices.* The contradiction, of course, is that even my resistance is a dead voice in anthropology. "Printed books are the habits of dead voices," said Bagese to Laundry. "The ear not the eye sees the stories."
ARL: *Dead Voices* is told, or rather the novel tells itself, as the visitation of the narrator, Laundry, to the old woman Bagese Bear in Oakland, California. Who is Bagese?
GV: Bagese is a name that comes from the *anishinaabe* language. *Bagese* means "to play a dish game," a game of wooden figures that are encouraged to stand in the dish by pitching the dish in a particular way. Bagese is a game of chance. The dish game is mentioned in many of my stories. Proude Cedarfair defeated Sir Cecil Staples, the monarch of gasoline, over a dish game in *Bearheart: The Heirship Chronicles.*
ARL: Games of chance are described in many of your books. You've said that *Dead Voices* is a game of chance called *wanaki.* How is that game played?
GV: The word *wanaki* in the *anishinaabe* language means "to live somewhere in peace," "to inhabit a place in peace," and by extension of that meaning, a chance of peace. The word *wanaki* is noted in the nineteenth-century *Dictionary of the Otchipwe Language* by Bishop Baraga but not in the recent *Concise Dictionary of Minnesota Chippewa* by John Nichols and Earl Nyholm. Bagese played *wanaki* as a game of chance, a tease of animal voices. She created a game of seven cards, and on each card was a picture, the

pose of a bear, beaver, crow, flea, squirrel, praying mantis, and the last card was the trickster, a wild card that turned the player into an animal or bird. So *wanaki* is a trickster game of chance, and she shows Laundry how to play this game. She turns each of the cards, and he tells the stories of the seven tricky chances. "Bagese, as you must have heard by now, became a bear last year in the city," wrote Laundry. "She is the same tribal woman who was haunted by stones and mirrors, and she warned me never to publish these stories or reveal the location of her apartment." My character in the novel, of course, tries to overcome the dead voices by telling the stories of the seven *wanaki* cards.

The game of peace is to take a chance on the real wherever you live and bring the real, the creatures, stones, leaves, insects, right into your life, rather than the poses of simulations, or the separations of dead voices. Bagese takes in the neighborhood, the real place where she lives near Lake Merritt in Oakland. She walks, she picks up small things here and there, a twig, a leaf, a stone, a feather. She picks up the universe that she sees and hears and encounters and carries these objects of chance to her apartment. There she places these memories of the real on the floor, in a picture of where she found them outside, and then creates a story about the real. So in this way she becomes the place of the story; she is the creation of the place.

ARL: Who is the narrator, Laundry?

GV: Laundry is not me, but he is a lecturer at the University of California. Bagese gave him that nickname because, she said, he smelled sweet like scented laundry soap. He is the carrier of dead voices. Laundry is tricky in his own way, and very persistent, but he lives by mere simulations. Bagese teased him about dead voices from the day they met near Lake Merritt. He had no connections to the real, no sense of presence, only reductive ideas that arose from the social sciences. Laundry, of course, was distracted by her tease, and very curious, but he could not at first understand her stories. Bagese was mysterious, and she outwitted him at every turn. She could easily tease him, but could she teach him and trick him out of his dead voices? She might have avoided such a character, he was so intense, so linear, so taken with cause and effect, so short on imagination, and yet he was the perfect student of a bear woman in the city. And yet, and yet, he creates the stories of Bagese.

ARL: She is a bear woman, and she becomes a bear. What is the significance? What is the importance of being a bear?

GV: We are bears, or we are teased by human bears. Bagese hears the voices of animals, and she moves in the memories and presence of bears. The mystery, of course, is that she could be seen in a mirror as a bear. Her game is to tease and convince people to take up the vision, the meditation and language of other lives, so they can create their own presence and sense of peace. She does so in the novel as she turns the *wanaki* cards in her apartment. And in this way she creates a chance of place, the stories of her presence as a bear.

ARL: Why especially a bear, though?

GV: Why? Because bears masturbate. Bears are tricky, and masturbate like humans. That makes sense because humans, in some native stories, are the heirs of bears. Humans are often outwitted by bears.

ARL: Bears are also very strong. Does that strength transfer to another kind of strength in Bagese? Does she, in other words, have visionary or shamanistic strength?

GV: Bears are very strong, but not necessarily in the way that most people think. Bears are strong because humans fear them, mostly. Bagese is a bear by creation, by memory, by meditation, by chance in her stories. She takes up the vision of the bear as her own. She is a human bear, and she scares other animals.

ARL: And her taking up the vision and becoming a bear, as you say, is linked to a cycle of charms, stones, bears (obviously), fleas, squirrels, mantises, crows, beavers, and finally tricksters. So in a way, she has a kind of serial identity. She becomes each of these with the turn of a card. Is that how you conceived of her in the novel?

GV: Bagese is a trickster in *Dead Voices*. She is, by memory and story, a mighty healer. She listens to birds and animals, and some people fear the sound of her stories. Bears scare many people, and so she poses as a bear on a park bench near Lake Merritt. She is a flea too, but who would fear a flea? Most people would sooner poison fleas than imagine their stories. Bagese creates the presence of squirrels, but most people think of squirrels as tricky rodents, even cute as they try to remember where they buried their nuts. Bagese is a trickster, and we are the animals that she creates in stories. She reminds the readers that we are animals, and that we are not separated by stories. She creates a sense of natural presence in the city.

ARL: Let me take you back to voices again. One of the observations that arise in the text is the following: "The secret, she told me, was not to pretend, but to see and hear the real stories behind the words, the voices of the animals in me." What do you mean by the "words"? What are these words?

GV: The heard stories are visual, a performance of words in visual memories. Once, in sound, the visual creation of stories come with the written words. I don't mean that the word is invested with an absolute visionary meaning. I mean that a reader teases the vision of words, the visual memories that arise in stories. Stories are not in the word, not in the printed word, but in the sound of memories. Readers may hear the vision of stories in the book, and that much is a trace of native creation. That, obviously, is more than the meaning of words. Bagese, for instance, travels out of ordinary time and place, and does so without a dictionary. Her moves and stories are visionary, in the presence of animals and birds and insects, and not by mere semantic turns. The difficulty here, of course, is in the choice of pronouns on the page. Laundry raises such questions because he does not understand the stories. I created this custodian of dead voices to be hunted in the stories of a bear woman. Naturally, that causes some tension over his mere presence, and challenges the idea that stories are visionary. He is hunted by a bear, and haunted by the mirrors, by his own absence in stories. Laundry might travel in the word, and in the dead voices, but he has no sense of presence in the visions of stories.

Somehow that anticipates the ideas of trace and deconstruction, of difference, that the meaning in a word is deferred to the next usage, to the next instance, or reference, or the next act of imagination in a story. There is that tease of the word, of course, but my idea of shamanic detection, natural reason, native memories, and visionary stories would surely be *detraced* by Jacques Derrida. I am not arguing that the word has an absolute meaning, or that there is any master writer or authority that gives the word meaning on the page, but the word is chance, a tease, and readers must hear creation and visual memory right into the book. Luther Standing Bear, for instance, is the tease of a visionary nickname. There are visual memories and stories of that name. The names are chance, of course, and the names are metaphors, and histories, and the names are visionary. The reader must hear the traces and stories of the names. Yes, the name may have ordinary meaning, a common trace, but there is more to the name than the lexical meaning. Standing Bear is a visionary story of a nickname given by native peers to describe the courage of the man who was given that name. This is a shadow distance, a shadow, not the author, that comes to the name in the book. That assumes, of course, that the reader can hear or read the shadows. My visual memories in stories are word cinemas, the shadow distance of my survivance. The times and places of creation are in stories, but not always in the written word. Maybe context is the cue, but the sound is what invites the visual memories in stories. The storiers, listeners, and readers come together in that shadow distance.

Now, of course, to say a word like Taurus, the constellation and the model of an automobile, is to visually recollect something quite simple, visual, and material. Even more could be created on a tour of the assembly line, the storied nicknames of an automobile. Then, of course, we must consider the zodiac and other shadow stories of Taurus. So the name has lexical meaning, but the rest is a creation of visual memory, a rich journey in the shadow distance of the name. Bagese creates chance in her stories. But then, her stories are the visionary lives of insects, the shadows of animals, birds, and tricksters, not the modern simulations of the Ford Motor Company.

ARL: Gerald, the shadows of meaning are a bit like the French word *rive*, which means "the edge of a river" and which gives us "arrive." Would that be like the shadows of a name?

GV: Yes, the tease and traces of a definition, and the shadows of visual memories in the stories of words. Bagese teases the dead voices with stories of how the words were used in visionary games. My stories tease a native presence at the treeline, at the shoreline, and that tease is similar to the meaning of the word *rive*, an edge, a shore, but not, of course, in the sense of margin, or separation.

Yes, *rive* as native survivance. And the meaning of the word *rive* and *riven* has yet another meaning in English. Bagese, then, is the *rive* of visionary stories.

ARL: Having mentioned a French source, let me mention another one, the great Samuel Beckett. How much was he on your mind when you wrote this novel?

GV: Beckett is always on my mind. *Dead Voices* starts with a quotation from *The Unnamable*. "Possessed of nothing but my voice, the voice," and at the threshold of his story there "will be the silence, where I am, I don't know, I'll never know, in the silence you don't know, you must go on, I can't go on, I'll go on." Bagese and her visions go on with me in the novel, in a native voice. Laundry, the narrator, ends the novel with these words: "We must go on."

Beckett is a greater writer, a master of the unnameable. I come to the world of literature with different experiences, of course, but his words go on in my imagination. The word is dead in the simulations of dominance, and there is no silence in nature. The sound of the voice is natural, a native tease at the *rive*, and the treeline, and yet our visionary memories are unnameable. Silence, though, is not the end of our stories. Beckett bears the shadows of James Joyce. They go to the pulse of names, visionary memories, and the creases of shamanic ironies. Beckett teases the silence, the absence, and he overturns the dead voices as he creates an unnameable sense of presence in his plays. I stand with him onstage, in the stocky, stubborn, tricky words of his characters, and say, "Beckett, we are at the threshold, the door opens, and we go on in our stories."

I write out of silence, and the unnameable, and the chance to create characters in the nick of time to hear me. Beckett is my obligation to say something, to go on. Bagese is there, in the tease of the novel, in the visionary voice of native reason. Beckett listens, in silence, and then he waves on the last words to other stories. We must go on. Silence is the tricky start, not the end of our stories. Bagese teases the academy of dead voices, the silence, and the curse of dominance. She turns to the mirror and we are bears. Beckett and Bagese are in the mirrors.

ARL: Is that Bagese's legacy, gift, inspiration?

GV: Bagese, I think, must have traveled with Beckett. Bagese might well have teased him as he came out of his house in Paris. She might have been waiting there as a crow, a flea, a human bear, to tease this delightfully awkward man. She might have teased his gait, the crease of his face, his look about, his pose of shyness on the street, the boldness of his eyebrows as he orders a drink. I imagine she teases the mighty writer over his punctuation, and she goes on as a bear, dressed as a waiter, to tease him at his favorite café. Bagese must tease his unnameable presence in my name.

ARL: And is she still teasing us?

GV: Naturally, as she must tease our conversation, and we are her best tease on that tricky road with the animals and Laundry. Bagese teased me at the very first silence, at that unnameable instance of my separation on the page. *Dead Voices*, in fact, comes out of that tricky tease of silence more than twenty years ago during my second winter quarter at the University of California, Berkeley. I could barely focus on anything that winter because there were demons in the water, in the mirrors, at every corner. I could hear the demons on the wind, and some of my enemies took advantage of my distraction. Minnesota was my escape distance, a great distance to imagine. I have always turned to nature when the page is cold and conversations cut to the soul. Bagese was there, and she teased me right back into the chance of my own story. I walked closer to the trees on my way to the campus. I sat in the eucalyptus with the squirrels, flew with the birds, and took care not to tread on anything, not even an ant. Bagese teased me as a Steller's jay.

I collected twigs, feathers, leaves, the traces of nature on my walks. Stones, bits of bark, string, wire, and even buttons. I created a map of my walks with these bits and pieces of nature, a tease of presence on the floor of my apartment. I blocked the demons at the door with these traces of nature. I chased madness out of my vision, and that became the *wanaki* game in my novel. Bagese teased me in the dish game. She created me as one of the figures in the game. She struck that mythic wooden dish on stone several times, and teased me, but my chance to stand was never easy. My father lost the game on his last chance in the city. I might have lost too, right here on the streets that winter in Berkeley. Bagese struck that dish on the stone four times to get me on my feet. My chance was in the nature around me, the bits and pieces of my survivance.

My notes, written in a fury, must have made sense at the time, but more than a decade later those images and comments became an unnameable document of my separation and, unpredictably, the start of my novel *Dead Voices*. I had created under stress, and in the presence of many demons that winter, the obscure notes on a narrative of survivance. Bagese, my grandmother, and a shadow of Nookomis were there to tease me, and so we created a *wanaki* game. The notes were a source of energy, but not even one sentence was carried to the novel. I wrote *Dead Voices* in one month, in a second fury that early summer just before Laura and I moved back to Berkeley from the University of Oklahoma. I had taught in the English Department there for one year, and then decided to return to the University of California. "Bagese," I said to myself after reading my notes several times and wondering why they should not be dumped, "we are going on a journey."

10

Almost Browne Stories

ARL: Now, another dish has been struck, namely, *Hotline Healers*, your Almost Browne novel. Who is he, and what is his world?

GV: My novel *Hotline Healers* came together with several obvious traces. The first trace is my short story "Hotline Healers: Virtual Animals on Panda Radio," which was published in *Caliban*. That story, about hotline connections to animal healers, is heard on talk radio. The second and most significant trace is the tricky baronage in *The Trickster of Liberty*. I turned once again to my favorite trickster characters in that novel and created new stories about their experiences on the reservations with Almost Browne. And the third trace is the narrative structure: a single trickster character, Almost Browne, presented in the voice of his curious cousin who travels with him to various universities. Almost, as you know, was almost born on the reservation. He is the son of Eternal Flame Browne, a native nun who renounced the convent and established a scapehouse on the barony. The narrator is the son of Father Mother Browne, a native priest who was once invested as a member of the Flat Earth Society in North Dakota. He returned to the reservation, renounced the priesthood, and opened a tavern named the Last Lecture. So the first person voice in *Hotline Healers* is Almost Browne's cousin, and he is almost a brother. This voice gives me a chance to tease the trickster and the reader. Almost told a newspaper reporter, "We live forever in stories, not manners, so, tease the chance of conception, tease your mother." And the trickster certainly did just that on his journey.

ARL: And is this told as a baronage journey?

GV: Yes, many of the scenes are told in tricky motion on the Naanabozho Express, the first native railroad on a reservation in this nation. And the ride was free, at last. The Naanabozho Express started at the Ozaawaa Casino Station on the White Earth Reservation and ran in a great circle to the baronage of Patronia and returned through the wild brush to the casino. So these stories are told on a native passenger train, and once the reader gets into the characters in the first few chapters of *Hotline Healers*, their tricky motion is carried out on a reservation railroad. Most of the characters on the train were active in previous scenes at the baronage. The Naanabozho Express becomes a native right of motion, and brings out the best in my characters, a natural sense of sovereignty. Almost's cousin, the narrator, would be my cousin too, a tricky turn of identities. The author, of course, is not the narrator, but he is a close cousin in this novel.

ARL: The train ride is a delight at every whistle stop. Did you turn around the railroads that were once built through reservations?

GV: Clement Hudon Beaulieu, my distant *anishinaabe* relative who was once an agent for the American Fur Company, built a home and trade center at old Crow Wing, Minnesota. My ancestor and his partners were certain that the railroad would be built right to their door, an obvious new station, but the route bypassed their land. Shortly thereafter my relatives were removed to the new White Earth Reservation. That first railroad, you might say, was a robber baron line.

ARL: So you established a trickster railroad?

GV: The Naanabozho Express was in my tricky native family. I was there, on a free ride to the casino, and my teeth were examined, and the mongrels had the run of the train. Everything, you see, was free. What a gift of travel, teeth, immaculate conceptions, and there for the asking in motion, in the parlor car on a native line. Now that is a real reservation, the right of motion, mongrels, and survivance. Almost Browne has that gift of motion, that natural tease, and an absolute sense of native sovereignty. First he imagines the world in the back seat of junk cars on the reservation, and then he takes up the book business, his first tricky enterprise, and hawks blank books out of the back of a station wagon in front of the English Department at the University of Minnesota. I might have done that, but instead took courses in literature. Almost had a better start than me, though, because he was paid huge honoraria to lecture at colleges and universities all over the country. Naturally, when he was not lecturing he sold copies of his fine blank books. And he signed these blank books in the names of famous authors, such as N. Scott Momaday and Ishmael Reed. Almost is a natural, dramatic speaker because, rather than studied speeches, he imagines the scenes, a tricky creation right onstage. Almost is absolutely charming, quite contradictory, and he is of a time and place that students praised as original and refreshing, a natural blank book educator.

Almost was, in fact, invited to deliver the commencement lecture at the Transethnic Situations Department at the University of California. Naturally, the faculty was troubled by his original stories and remarks, and they rightly assumed the students were getting even at last. Almost was offensive but humorous, evasive but pleasurable, in that tricky sense of associations, and he said something to offend everyone. The faculty turned into academic party poopers and, one by one, abandoned the commencement. The students resisted the trickster tease, as best they could, but natural reason is more convincing than objectivism. The students shouted at the trickster, challenged him, and in the end hissed at him, but my cousin stood to deliver a tricky, honorable critique of higher, or was it a lower, transethnic education. Almost overcame the counter comments with visionary stories, and at last, hundreds of students removed their black gowns as an act of liberation. The ethnic students gave up the ghost of medieval mimicry.

ARL: There's a lot about dentistry in these stories. Why so?

GV: Many natives have trouble with their teeth, and native smiles show more than one story. Good teeth might point to adoption, a mission, or at least to a better-than-average family. So an important native service on any reservation is dental care. Gesture Browne, for that reason, became an acudenturist and treated people on the Naanabozho Express. Gesture was given the seven-coach railroad train, in fact, because he had saved the life of a banker and his grandson in a storm on Lake Namakan. Gesture is a meditative acudenturist, and a native visionary. Some natives said he was a shaman dentist. He pulled, filled, and polished teeth, and he fitted native dentures for free on the train. The banker, before he turned over his private railroad, had an expensive dental chair installed in the parlor car. Gesture, our great uncle, created signature false teeth, original tricky native smiles.

ARL: The Browne family has been an ongoing interest and an imagined world in your writing. Do you intend to go on with the Brownes as a family, or as a dynasty?

GV: The Baron of Patronia has been with me in many, many stories. My baronage cousins taught me how to overturn manifest manners, and how to live in motion, a natural sovereignty. Alice Beaulieu, my grandmother, would have liked our cousins on the baronage, although she would certainly have teased me about the hot springs. Almost Browne would tease her right back. My grandmother and father probably would have recognized most of my characters.

Hotline Healers is my last collection of stories about the trickster family from the baronage. These characters, as you pointed out, are in several stories and in The Trickster of Liberty. They have also been characters in other novels. The stories in Hotline Healers gather them all together, and the bright leader is Almost Browne. This is the last of these trickster stories. My next novels will focus on natives elsewhere in the world, in Germany, England, Japan, and China. I have already done that, of course, in Griever: An American Monkey King in China. Griever de Hocus will be back once more. My interest now is to write stories that place natives in historical situations around the world. The Baron of Patronia and Almost Browne are close to a tricky retirement on the Naanabozho Express.

ARL: Some time ago a spat broke out between Leslie Silko and Louise Erdrich about the oral and scriptural divide in native writing. You yourself have spoken about a new native literary war. What do you have in mind?

GV: Michael Dorris once posed as the mannerly, essential voice of native literature, and for many years he managed a significant enterprise of novels and motion pictures in the family. He and his wife, Louise Erdrich, published several books and won many prizes, and their success, of course, attracted some distant envy. Michael and Louise were a charming couple, but their literary persona did not please some natives. That hardly mattered, because they were established in New York City. Michael carried on one of the first postindian literary wars, in a sense, by his aesthetic cruises among agents, editors, publishers, and others in the book industry, by his identity apologies, by his academic poses, and by his dominance of other native authors. He accused me, for instance, of saying bad things about his wife's novel, *The Beet Queen*. He wrote to me about the matter and declared that the native literary world was too small to carry on criticism of each other. He was right about that, it is too *small* a world, but he was wrong to accuse me of what seemed to be a rather generous critical thought, hardly worthy of a stern warning. The criticism, in fact, was not mine, but the comments of a mutual friend who had done nothing more than mention the fact that Leslie Silko, author of *Ceremony*, had written a critical review of Erdrich's novel in the *Albuquerque Journal*. Silko praised the "smooth style" of the novel and noted that Erdrich's prose was "dazzling and sleek," although the tribute seemed to be ironic. Dorris, more often than not, strained to speak for his wife, and he must have been terribly preoccupied with the family enterprises to be bothered by so slight a comment in a review. Maybe what angered him the most was Silko's criticism that *The Beet Queen* was a "strange artifact" because the novel rarefied the pain and poverty of North Dakota. Louis Owens discusses the review in *Other Destinies*. Silko, he said, seemed to focus on the notion that natives must write about natives, and left little to the diversity of culture. So that seems to be one of the teases of the first literary war.

The second postindian literary war has been carried on by Elizabeth Cook-Lynn. She poses as a great and grumpy scholar of native literature, but her critical comments are rather narrow, separatist, and essentialist, at times, as she sets out to reconstruct the postindian notions of a traditional past. She seems very determined to become the grand arbiter of native identity, of who is, who might be, and who is not a *real* native author. Cook-Lynn must be a very clever shaman to know the real from the other, but such modernist concoctions are the obvious traces of racial separatism. She could be the conservative elder regent of *true* prairie stories, and in that sense she would never survive the tease of a trickster creation. Yes, and the arbiters of the authentic wear so many masks to carry out the literary blues of racial exclusions. Sadly, separatism seems to be the demonic crease of these literary wars.

Sherman Alexie, who seems to be obsessed with the politics of terminal identity, declared the third literary war in native literature. He is critical, for some obscure reason, of native authors who do not live on or near reservations, and yet, as he strains for tradition he writes back the stories of simulations and silhouettes. Alexie poses close to the ancient bones, but is his pose a nostalgia for victimry? He clicks an electronic mouse with a common touch, creates postindian stories, and then scorns other authors. These are tiresome *indian* poses in the literary wars.

Who has the right to be a native? Who has the right to write about *indians* and natives? How much native blood does it take to be a real *indian* author? The answers to these questions vary from war to war, but the accusations always come down to racialism, separatism, and cultural dominance. Native blood is not the same as experience or imagination, and the metaphor of native blood is certainly not measured by the liter or even the reservation colonial pint. Most of these postindian word warriors and identity inquisitors have it wrong, very wrong, and they've had it wrong longer than anyone in the country. Fittingly, *The Stranger*, a weekly newspaper in Seattle, recently referred to Sherman Alexie as the Shermanator.

There are, in spite of the identity inquisitors, many smart, dedicated, strong historians and interpreters of native literature. LaVonne Ruoff and Karl Kroeber are the most distinguished of the literary historians. Ruoff has, in her many publications, established the serious study of native literature. Kroeber initiated, and for many years edited, *Studies in American Indian Literatures*, the only scholarly journal in the country dedicated to the study of native literature. Alan Velie, as you know, was one of the first literary scholars to consider native literature in a comparative context, and he did so almost twenty years ago with the publication of *Four American Indian Literary Masters*. Louis Owens, in his original, outstanding book *Other Destinies*, has advanced the study of native authors as literary artists. Ruoff, Kroeber, Velie, Owens, and many others have presented native literature as a creative art, not as a culture artifact. In the past, as you know, so many interpreters carried out that long-standing influence of the social sciences. That is to say, everything in literature serves some cultural object, and that objectivism is a simulation of the social sciences. The cultural artifact approach has been a terrible burden not only for writers but also for interpreters and teachers because they feel as if they cannot teach native literature without some social science knowledge of the culture, as if, in fact, the author simulated such ridiculous and mundane reductions of culture in the creation of a poem or novel. Louis Owens has made it positively impossible to turn back on the serious critical study of native literature.

Robert, you too have taken great care to present literature, native and other literature, as a literary art. I have heard you many times touch the very heart of literary creation with your generous humor and original comments, and you tease the pleasurable, comparative connections in the history of literature. Arnold Krupat has advanced the interpretations of native literature in similar but more theoretical ways.

Listen, to turn this conversation around, there is more than mere love in the consideration of native literature, and you know that better than anyone. There is always doubt, deception, postindian trickeries, but who can bear the inquisition separatists? The demons of absence, and always the envious, turn to victimry. Even the tease of hate, as love and hate are never opposites, is a sense of presence and survivance. John Berger, the novelist, wrote in *And Our Faces, My Heart, Brief as Photos* that the "opposite of to love is not to hate, but to separate." I know you've heard me quote that before, but it seems important to repeat it now. Love, hate, and irony are a common bond, but not separations. We are sustained by love, hate, and tricky stories of survivance. So the serious considerations of native literature as literary arts are touched and teased by love, hate, irony, and tricky stories, but not by manifest manners or victimry. Only the identity inquisitors are into the blood politics of envy and separations.

ARL: In this respect, perhaps one could mention the Native American Literature Prize you initiated at the University of California, and the American Indian Literature and Critical Studies Series, for which you are the general editor, at the University of Oklahoma Press. I understand the prize has not been awarded for some years, although the series itself has been extremely successful.

GV: The Native American Literature Prize was established as an annual award for an outstanding native author. I initiated the prize at the University of California, Santa Cruz. The first prize was awarded to N. Scott Momaday in 1989. The second annual prize was given to Paula Gunn Allen. Then James Welch was awarded the third annual prize at the University of Oklahoma. I had accepted the David Burr Chair of Letters, an endowed position in the English Department, and the literary prize was generously supported by the provost, Joan Wadlow, of the University of Oklahoma. The annual prize should have continued there with foundation endowments, but the proposal was tortured by various agents and finally strangled to death in academic politics. The proposal, at the time, was to present the prize every other year, and the administration would be carried out by the director and editor of *World Literature Today*. The enemies of the prize resisted the idea that native literature was international. James Welch was the last author to receive the annual Native American Literature Prize. At about the same time, Willis Regier, who was then director of the University of Nebraska Press, invited me to consider a prose award for native authors. So we established the annual North American Indian Prose Award, and that series of publications continues with great success.

The American Indian Literature and Critical Studies Series was founded at about the same time as the demise of the prize. Kimberly Wiar, an acquisitions editor at the University of Oklahoma Press, encouraged me to propose a new series that would celebrate native literature and critical studies. My idea was that there should be a literary series as distinguished as the American Indian Civilization Series. My proposal was approved by the editors, and two years later the first book published in our series was a novel, *The Sharpest Sight*, by Louis Owens, in 1992. At the moment we have published about thirty outstanding novels and critical studies in the series, including *Firesticks* by Diane Glancy, *On Native Ground* by Jim Barnes, and *The Light People* by Gordon Henry. The general objective of the series is to publish original fiction and criticism that envisions a new presence of natives in the world, rather than serving the interests of social science to carry out, once again, the traditions of past cultures.

11

Visionary Sovereignty

ARL: You consider the "native theaters" of identity and the troubles of separation and victimry in *Fugitive Poses: Native American Indian Scenes of Absence and Presence*. What, then, are these native theaters?

GV: Consider me one of the native theaters, along with my father, who moved from the White Earth Reservation. I created eight theaters of native relations, or sources of identities and connections of inheritance. The title of my book *Fugitive Poses* is a metaphor of these theaters of identity. My assurance of the theaters, you see, is that natives and especially *indians* have always had an audience.

The eight theaters are about the dramatic traces of native memories, about the causes of connections and separations and, obviously, the nasty and treasonous business of racial blood quanta. The theaters, in an aesthetic sense, are the piecemeal estates of native identity. We imagine ourselves in the presence of an audience, and that means there are many native estates of survivance. I wrote about only eight of the many public theaters of identity in *Fugitive Poses*. These connections are stories of *indians* by concession, natives by creation, countenance, genealogies, actual situations, trickster stories, and identity by victimry. I mean, in the theater of concession, that everyone must be included as an *indian*, and that because the name is a simulation in the first place. So we should include everyone as an *indian* who so desires and, once and for all time, get past the racial accusations and separations over a colonial simulation. Natives have everything to gain and nothing to lose by this concession, by embracing others in a linguistic slave name. Why not include Jaime de Angulo, Lynn Andrews, Carlos Castaneda, and Jamake Highwater in a name that has more to do with them as *indians* than natives?

The estate of natives by creation would include those writers and artists who have imagined characters and scenes with such aesthetic power. Gary Snyder, the poet, John Neihardt, the visionary listener who transcribed *Black Elk Speaks*, and even James Fenimore Cooper would be native by their creations. Karl May, the German author, has been active in two theaters and might be both native by creation and *indian* by the force of his simulations. Surely, embracing these artists is more pleasurable in the context of comparative literature than picking the old wounds of separation and vengeance. The theater of countenance is obvious by appearance, manners, and other native features and traces of identity. So what are the other theaters? Native by genealogy is one of the obvious connections, and so is a document, such as a birth certificate, boarding school record, and enrollment on reservation. Native by situation is an earned connection by individuals who are honored by native communities. Consider the Jewish traders who married natives and became leaders in Pueblos. Native by trickster stories is the most obscure and at the same time the most creative. This connection would embrace some politicians, say, for instance, President John Kennedy, Hubert Humphrey, and Walter Mondale, who carried on in headdress, tricky peace pipes, and yet served more often than not the good sense of natives.

The last estate is the most common, the theater of victimry. The grand leader of natives by victimry is Ward Churchill, but ironically, he serves a rather modernist cause of victimry. The theater of native victimry, it seems, attracts the largest but not always the most active audience. Churchill, no doubt, would object to most of my theater scenes, and he might misread the reproduction of a painting by David Bradley on the cover of *Fugitive Poses*. Bradley's a brilliant, ironic *anishinaabe* artist, and this new painting, *Ghost Dance Revelations*, is a visionary resurrection of natives. Bradley never plays to the theater of victimry. Churchill, on the other hand, is the master player of native victimry. The last estate, and ninth native theater, is futurity. There, but not in *Fugitive Poses*, the ninth theater and casinos are closed for the season.

ARL: Can a university press series, such as the one you initiated, compete with the best-seller syndrome of publishers in New York?

GV: Robert, the series considers the publication of original native
        stories and critical studies, as you know, and not trendy con-
        sumer titles in a mass market economy. So far the books in the
        series have been favorably reviewed, and the authors praised for
        their literary talents. Yes, and most of the books in the series
        have sold reasonably well, but not in competition with mass
        market publishers. As the series grows so do the readers, and with
        that more favorable attention to the new books published in the
        series. There's an obvious pleasure to be published in a series that
        has such a good reputation. My view, in the context of original
        native literature, is that most best-seller books about natives
        must satisfy common *indian* simulations. My focus here is on
        consumer fiction, not history, because the common fantasies of
        readers about *indians* are continuations of the concocted adven-
        tures of captivity narratives. There are exceptions, of course, but
        the fantasies of a bourgeois consumer culture cannot be ignored
        by mass market publishers. My interest is to encourage serious
        literary artists who create new myths and stories about natives
        in diverse situations, and who do not solely rest on *indian* simu-
        lations or romantic revisions of traditions to move a character.

ARL: Are there implications here about the translation and publication
        of native texts in other countries?

GV: Yes, the *indian* best-sellers are much easier to represent to agents
        in international literary markets, but that, of course, does not
        make for an easy translation. The readers are there, and so are
        the expectations of *indian* simulations, but not creative native
        cultures. Readers everywhere are ready, by way of constant simu-
        lations, to encounter familiar *indians* in literature, the romantic
        indians in themes of savagism and civilization. The German
        novelist Karl May, for instance, created *indian* warriors at the
        turn of the last century that are so familiar that translations
        of original native stories must now embrace some of the same
        simulations to reach most readers. Since early colonial contact
        the translation of native stories has been a serious problem,
        and that's especially troublesome, as you know, if the characters
        and situations are not simulations of *indians* that readers easily
        recognize. The most visionary native stories are not as familiar
        as the *indian* simulations. Not only that, but most of the books
        published in our series are visionary and more diverse in structure

and imagery than any *indian* simulations in consumer literature. Generally, these literary qualities might make translation more complicated, and expensive, but apparently this has not been a problem in the translation of a novel in the series by Louis Owens, *The Sharpest Sight*, which was recently published in France.

ARL: Since you yourself have mentioned postmodernism, and with it the idea of the postindian, what of the older representations of the "Indian" in popular culture and literature?

GV: Christopher Columbus and his rogues carved the name *indian* on a cruise, a new slave name of discovery, and here we are in conversation, five centuries later, or are we in servitude to the metes and bounds of *indian* simulations? That sounds much too clever. Yes, yes, the semantic slaves bear that name, the *indian*, and at the same time, the name invites our evasion and resistance. So the postindian names, in an ironic sense, are the actual names of native creation, such as *anishinaabe*, that transpose the *indian* simulations.

I mention many native names in my books that are not as familiar to readers as *indian* slave names and manifest manners, that is, the modern manners that have carried out the notions of manifest destiny. I teased that idea, as you know, in *Manifest Manners: Postindian Warriors of Survivance*. The word *indian*, for instance, is the most common simulation of manifest manners. Actually, you know about my insistence that the word be printed in italics. Consider the burden of the name *indian*, and other names that modify the simulation, such as *chippewa indian*. The natives who must bear these names are known, in their own language, as the *anishinaabe*. Obviously, the name *indian* perpetuates manifest manners and cultural dominance. The native authors who overturn these simulations create a postindian literature, that is, an original literature that rises out of the manifest manners of rogues and empires. There's more to postindian consciousness than mere resistance, but those native authors who take pleasure in tricky stories and deconstruct the authority of simulated names are never easy to translate. The *indian* is ironic, to be sure, and a conveyance of manifest manners. Natives must overturn the simulations of the *indian* and leave the treasons of that slave name to the arbiters of colonial authenticity.

ARL: Which brings us to television and movies. How do you regard the handling of native cultures, native politics, native experience in these most seductive, most powerful media?

GV: My views waver over the extremes of the arts and entertainment, and the power of movie simulations. One extreme is that these *indian* simulations have become the *real*, and they influence people, positively and negatively. Movies change stories, distract memories, and invite viewers to substitute their own experiences, or the tease of their own experience, for something more glamorous and impressive on the screen. *Dances with Wolves* is a romantic, positive simulation, a beautiful movie story that satisfies every stereotype you could imagine about *indians* on screen. Once more, as in *Little Big Man*, the movies create new romantic *indian* simulations by way of an adventurous white man. Consider how an original postindian script might overtake the simulations in any movie. *Dances with Wolves* and *Little Big Man* would become ironic movie stories in a postindian production. The ironies might even double because most audiences would resist the tease of simulations. So play the usual popular simulations for the audience, or turn tricky and postindian and the ironies are lost on most audiences. I mean enormous audiences, great box office hits, not the pleasures of art theater audiences. The romantic warriors of *Dances with Wolves* and *Little Big Man*, and a few other movies, are the savages in the structural theme of savagism and civilization, but the simulations were reversed at the end of the Vietnam War. Overnight, the native warriors are the metaphors of civilization, and the soldiers of manifest destiny are the demonic savages. That wicked war, of course, has reversed much more than the prosaic themes of civilization in the movies. Reversed civilizations or not, we know what happens to *indians* at the end of the movies. They vanish, as the tragic simulations of *indians* must do in the movies, because their absence is better understood than their presence. Even so, many native actors take pleasure in playing *indians* in the movies, and that could be another postindian irony. The production of *Dances with Wolves* in South Dakota has inspired new simulations or romantic warriors, and has increased the number of *indian* actors and native technicians. All of these new movie stories are positive and romantic at the moment, but they are, nevertheless, simulations of *indians*, and that means the image is an invention with no connection or referent to the real. Simulations deliver popular stereotypes, and they are very familiar messages, very powerful. I would, of course, much rather be a romantic simulation of a warrior than a demonic savage in the movies. Yes, *Dances with Wolves* is grand and gorgeous, and even the horses are magnificent, but you know, the horses cast no shadows in that movie.

The other extreme is violence, and simulations of *indians* as an absence, but wait, the choice of some simulations is much easier than others. Who, in their right mind, would not choose the romance of warriors over separation and victimry? Yet some extremes in the movies turn ironic with time, as the romance cuts right to the funny bone, and the tragic becomes the comic, as in *Broken Arrow* or even *Soldier Blue*. These natural revisions, so to speak, or the ironies of extreme time, are other aspects of postindian considerations. On the one hand, every scene about *indians* in the movies must be postindian, because the scenes are edited after many takes, and there might be several hundred people working on the set, such as writers, editors, and camera, sound, and light technicians. Maybe, at last, the very best *indian* scenes in the movies are postindian, and that might be the best of our entertainment. So, could the old *indians* of the westerns be the new postindian ironies played out in the dark at the movies? Casinos, no doubt, could become the new western sets of postindian sovereignty.

ARL: What about documentary films? Are there any advances to be found in films like *Thunderheart* or *Incident at Oglala?*

GV: The *indian*, not natives, is the object of these and other films. The simulations of the other, the *indian* as absence, are what seems to satisfy most movie audiences, not the presence of natives with all their diversity and contradictions. The *indian* documentary should be ironic, but as you know, the simulations are much too popular. So the *indian*, or the radical *indian* of political victimry, could be the ironic rather than the essential object of a movie documentary. Now, for all that, what is a documentary? *Thunderheart* and *Incident at Oglala* are factual manners, or the dramatic scenes of objectivity, and in this sense, documentaries are promotions, advertisements, and propaganda. Movies are entertainment, edited stories, not *true* representations of anything. These documentary movies, and many others, are in the tragic mode, in the sense that they are an imitation of action, as Aristotle might say, rather than of people, and that arouses emotions. But most movies strive to deliver at least that much in the dark. Movies, documentary propaganda or not, are created out of memories, histories, and what else? The tic and turns of audiences? Obviously, *indians* or not, irony or victimry, movies are scripted, directed, acted, shot, and edited, and such creations are not mere representations. To say that documentaries are the tragic imitations of true *indian* experiences would authenticate nothing more than manifest manners and dominance. Documentary movies on *indians* are either in the tragic mode and ironic, or scenes of victimry.

ARL: Russell Means has won your admiration, at times, for what may be his unintended irony. What of the coopting of a figure like Means in films like *The Last of the Mohicans?*

GV: Consider Russell Means as a postindian hostage of James Fenimore Cooper. Now, that would be a mighty documentary. Means has always been an actor, a man at the mirror, captured by his own political image, and a very aggressive leader in convincing others to participate in his plays. Obviously, he would not call his radical poses mere play. True, the acts of a movie warrior are much more serious. Means might turn a revolution into a documentary, but how could he resist the simulations of his *indian* presence and, in that sense, his *real* absence? On the other hand, he has actively promoted animated cartoons as *indian* representations in the movie *Pocahontas.* You know, talking trees, and the countenance of a gorgeous *indian* maiden. Means, you know, once demonstrated against the movie *A Man Called Horse* because it depicted *indians* as savages. Yes, it must be true, tough guys and postindian warriors are touched by the virtual reality of animated *indians* in the movies.

ARL: Do you see Russell Means, Clyde Bellecourt, Ward Churchill, and others as "acting" their parts in the politics of the American Indian Movement?

GV: The American Indian Movement, as you know, is a recent *indian* production in the course of native resistance, and most of the reviews of this revisionary *indian* production are evasive, to say the least. Natives have a long history of resistance, and that resistance has been political, moral, and visionary. Think about the Pueblo Revolt, Geronimo and the resistance of the Chiricahua Apaches, and the Ghost Dance religion. So, what are you asking me about the American Indian Movement? Do these actors have a sense of history and humor? Would these extreme actors have a cause without federal and church grants? Russell Means might well have invented the radical *indian* money wheel, but that does not necessarily mean that his forceful performances in politics and movies are visionary. Ward Churchill seems to be an ideologue of *indian* victimry, and as a consequence, he lacks a sense of native irony. The *indian* is a media simulation, an absence, not a presence or resistance, and while simulations hold court in popular culture they have never amounted to much as a native connection or constituency.

Natives are storiers, and humor is a touchstone of native presence, so who can present the stories and humor of the American Indian Movement? The best native stories are not about victimry. Dennis Banks, for instance, another very fine actor, was once teased for his many *my heart is heavy, my pocket book is empty* speeches to the good liberals of Minnesota. Clyde Bellecourt, another hard-edge ideologue of *indian* victimry, was convicted in federal court and sentenced to five years in prison for the distribution of drugs. I wrote about his abuses of authority and the law in *Manifest Manners*. Bellecourt was not sentenced to a federal prison for his culture, courage, or conscience, as were many native resistance fighters more than a century ago. He was a drug dealer, and there's nothing strong or manly about that in native experiences.

So many of the movement actors pose as stoical *indians*, a romantic pose once celebrated by the photographer Edward Curtis. Surely, some *indians* live a good life by their poses. Sadly, though, others count their rights to casino sovereignty. You know, none of this would seem so mundane, or even so absurdly prescriptive, if the players took some pleasure in their own theater or ironies. Yes, an *indian* theater, not a native trickster story. Maybe we could encourage a wiser humor in a new vaudeville *indian* movement. There is so much humor to bear in the simulations of dominance.

ARL: Ward Churchill recently blew up at you and alleged, in a review of your book *Manifest Manners*, that your views of tribal life and culture were, in his words, "obscurantist, rhetorical." I'm sure you have a response.

GV: Ward Churchill is the master obscurantist, so he ought to know his names. He cries *indian* victimry, but his academic poses are revisionary modernism, and that leaves him without much humor or irony. He raves at racial silhouettes, but in this case, he raves at my book because he would have been more malicious about the federal narcotics conviction of Clyde Bellecourt.

ARL: Gerald, allow me to persist, because Ward Churchill bills himself as a radical tribal leader. He has written voluminously on tribal history and tribal politics, and he has done so from a Marxist position. Has he got it all wrong?

GV: Karl Marx and his teasers need a native vision. Marxism, in the course of native stories, is revisionary, not visionary. Churchill is an academic power player, a modernist, and his reactions are bound more to *indian* victimry than native survivance. His simulations are very shrewd, but not wrong. Even so, his signature is victimry, and the politics of that is not right in native stories. Churchill is radically minded, to be sure, but his personal anger does not make him a nat.ve leader.

ARL: Where, then, is that leadership to be found? Or is leadership itself a simulation, or a redundancy?

GV: Natives have always been traders, tricky storiers, and visionaries, so there is no obvious sacred or secular connection to *indian* victimry. Native leaders arise in communities and show their stuff in ordinary situations, and in the politics of their visions, and of course, by their courage and resistance. Black Elk, for instance, held back the story of his vision until he was certain the politics were right and he would be accepted as a leader. Can you imagine yesterday's kitschy radicals holding back a vision? The *indian* is an institutional construction, not a vision of native authority or direction, and the emergence of the new media *indian* is a romantic simulation of tragic victimry. That conversion is hardly visionary.

How could an *indian* pose as a leader? A leader of what — simulations of an absence? The issues of leadership are so complex, and the sources of power and contradictions are so diverse, that the references to natives, or traditional sources of responsibility, are often obscured by the demands of economies, casinos, resources, and federal connections. In that same sense it would be stupid to define or generalize the characteristics of *indian* or native leaders. Natives are much too complicated, not only because of the diversities of native languages and communities, but diverse by religion, associations with political parties, education, class, age, state, and urban or reservation economies. Similarly, we cannot easily describe the virtues of native leaders, except to say the obvious: integrity, community service, and responsibility. Many leaders are created, but who are the creators? Who creates native and *indian* leaders? Native storiers, visionaries, and communities, or the media and academic institutions?

ARL: And yet names there are. And in the last few years we've seen figures like Senator Ben Nighthorse Campbell of Colorado, the many dedicated native lawyers, and the distinguished name of Vine Deloria. How do you think of their contributions?

GV: Robert, you started this part of the conversation by asking me about the politics and leadership of the American Indian Movement. Again, the complexities of native service and responsibility are such that we cannot easily generalize the meaning of leadership. Yet the demands on leaders are so great, and often contradictory, that failure is almost expected in many cases. Corruption is widespread, especially now, with the riches of casinos and the envy of the politics of monied power. There are many leaders, native and *indian*, as you point out, but who can easily name the categories of leadership? Vine Deloria has been active as a leader of native organizations, as a national advocate, and as a very distinguished writer and philosopher for more than forty years. Senator Campbell is heard in many worlds. Obviously, natives reach out to those who are visionaries, who are strong, wise in politics, and those who have earned recognition as professionals, such as native medical doctors, lawyers, artists, bankers, and technicians, and make use of their services. That is a right of consciousness and a grant of integrity. But the idea of a leader is much more elusive than service. Leaders are named, elected, trusted, and mistrusted, and the politics are real, simulated, and visionary. Sometimes, because of the actual issues at hand, and the politics of survivance, the best of the real might be an *indian* simulation. Casinos and moneybags politics, new museums and postindian traditions, Mother Earth and water rights, the hands and gloves of *indian* simulations, are such ironies of the *real* in native communities. Natives and *indians* might stand alike by their casinos. Casinos could be the new fur trade, and who are the real leaders of this economic conversion?

ARL: I want to let that lead into another kind of politics, gender politics. Do you have a view of what has been called Indian feminism and the role played by, say, Paula Gunn Allen?

GV: Paula Gunn Allen has a rich sense of humor, and she is admired as a charismatic and tricky artist. She's generous, witty, complicated, and a strong creative writer. So, the politics of that are generous too, and in my view, she constructs an *indian* feminism out of modernity. Yes, her original thoughts and theories are very complex, because, it seems to me, she has converted a native sense of survivance into a rather modernist notion of gender. So what does that mean? Well, maybe she has actually converted a modernist conceit of *indian* gender, or the simulations of gender, into her own theories of "tribal gynocracies." *Modernism* may not be her word, but she does play the mythic to objective reason, and by tricky contentions, she somehow weaves arcane traditions into a new feminist enlightenment. That gynocratic notion, it seems to me, is an essentialist and a structural reversal of patriarchy. I doubt, however, that she would ever stand by any single theory. Not mine, and she certainly would not accept my critique. Even so, she has created a revisionist culture. I mean, she has created a culture of nurturance to advance a structural theory of gender, and that is a modernist absence of natives. Here and there in *The Sacred Hoop* she reverts to the notion of a native mystique, but mostly by way of objective reason. Paula might agree that gender is a native mystery, and with that a great irony arises from her tricky prose.

ARL: How do you see sovereignty, the custody of children, adoption, casinos, and related issues in native communities?

GV: Robert, who could answer that serious, generous summary? Each point you mention is an ongoing discussion in every native community. None of these issues are unilateral, because natives, obviously, are no longer isolated on federal exclaves. Reservations, yes, but not without an active sense of their own political futurity.

Sovereignty and child welfare are significant issues of the family, but they are also legal, political, and cultural issues of entire native communities. Many of these issues must be negotiated in institutions and others argued in courts. The family is always the source of solace and trouble, of course, but nothing has been that obvious since natives were removed to reservations.

The care and protection of native children takes love, humor, and institutions to provide health and education. Casinos take integrity, tricky negotiations, and a visionary dedication to humanitarian causes, otherwise envy might overcome the sudden riches. Casinos are at the very heart of native sovereignty. Reactive modernism is envy politics and the curse of native sovereignty, and for that reason, casino reservations must become active in international humanitarian issues, such as the support of stateless families. Why not make an active stand for stateless children in the world? Why not? Because of greed and corruption in the management of many reservation casinos. So greed and envy could be the end of native sovereignty. Casinos could easily support active and honorable natives to negotiate a humanitarian position in the world, and to work with other nations and international organizations in the interest of children and families. The world would honor the natural reason and wisdom of natives. Why not support the children and stateless families of Kurdistan and Tibet? What more can be said but to shame those who may, by their very greed and the envy of others, be responsible for the slow, ignoble death of native sovereignty.

There are many other issues that are being negotiated in native communities and argued in court every day. These are issues that arise over native water rights, over the reserved rights doctrine, over resources, over sacred sites, over the return of human remains and sacred objects, and over treaties. More and more serious issues arise over land use, the disposal of nuclear waste, and one of the most haunting legacies of native service to this country, the hundreds of miners and their families who were poisoned by nuclear mining in Arizona and New Mexico.

ARL: The New Age interests, uses, and misuses of native legacies are not really so new. Why has this literary indulgence raised your hackles?

GV: My critique is ironic, as it must be, but not always. Those who pose as healers bother me the most, but not those who claim some esoteric vision. Carlos Castaneda creates great stories but has never posed as a healer. Lynn Andrews, you know, creates a romantic healer high in the mountains, who indeed healed the author – to the tune of hundreds of thousands of dollars from the sales of her books. The fiction is great, and the rest is a simulation that promotes the absence of natives. To create *indians* as some strain of true wisdom derived from arcane healers in hidden places is a deception, but this is not the first time, of course, that publishing has made millions on simulations and deceptions.

The New Age movement is a market courtesy. Yes, and the courtesy, in turn, embraces an *indian* mystery. Yet the only real mystery, it seems to me, is why the sale of books by native authors has never been as great as by those who write about *indian* simulations. Obviously, readers are better acquainted with the simulations of an *indian* absence than with the presence of natives in original stories. These simulations serve an eager audience, and many writers deliver *indian* simulations without a trace of irony. Lynn Andrews, and many other authors, such as the healer dealers of the *indian* romance, are not visionaries. They are courtesy authors of a market that promotes *indian* simulations. The tragic stories of an *indian* absence are worth more to publishers than a real native sense of presence and survivance.

"I have a great vision, and my *indian* teacher lives alone on a sacred mountain." That simple statement would not necessarily be rewarded in the ordinary world, and certainly not in a native community. However, in New Age California, such a confession, even as a possession, could be the focus of a radio or television talk show and, soon enough, a book contract. The author may have had a vision, but that does not mean that a vision of *indian* simulations could heal anyone but a needy reader. Native visions are not empowered by agents or publishers. The native vision and the cure must have a constituency. The vision must, indeed, earn an audience, and that, you know, means the dynamic politics of a native community. Now, who is responsible for *indian* simulations and fake cures? The authors, of course. But the reader should demand at least a sense of irony.

ARL: Gerald, what you seem to be describing is really a step back in native history. Do you mean Wovoka, the Ghost Dance religion, and that kind of vision?

GV: The Ghost Dance religion, as you know, is not a step back in any history. Wovoka envisioned a mighty dance of souls, of ghosts in a native resurrection, and that story is more than history. That vision is a creative connection, the instance of ecstatic motion. The Ghost Dance is natural reason and transmotion; that is, the resurrection dance is a visionary motion of sovereignty. Many native stories and novels are visionary, a literary dance of ghosts. *House Made of Dawn* by N. Scott Momaday, and *Ceremony* by Leslie Silko, and *Medicine River* by Thomas King, and *Bone Game* by Louis Owens, and many others, are visionary novels.

ARL: Could we turn back to the issue of casinos, to the ownership and corruption of reservation casinos? There's a whole spectrum of things there that play into the controversies. Have you yourself ever wanted to own or run a casino?

GV: Absolutely, and what a fabulous idea, to manage a casino. My first act would be to give at least half of the profits to international programs, in the name of native humanity – you know, my proposal to serve stateless children and families in the world. I would also use some of the casino money to establish the first native embassy. Where, you might ask? Well, probably in the Middle East.

My response has been much too serious, so back to the reservation games. I think it would be great fun to wear cowboy boots and a turquoise bolo tie and parade around a casino as a manager of the games. Who could have imagined that some *indians* would become rich by reservation casinos? I mean rich, and the envy of rich, not enriched. Think of it, the players are bent over the tables and machines, ever so determined to lose, yes, *lose*, and the manager, and that's me, sweeps through the room with a smile, and wise gestures, teasing the ultimate losers to play more and more. What a fantastic deal, and that because of treaties. I mean, are these casinos some sort of trickster creation story?

I wrote a story in my recent book, *Hotline Healers*, about a casino that is taken over by a trickster tornado on the White

Earth Reservation. The funnel of that tornado passed right over the casino and sucked the coins out of every machine. Millions of quarters were sucked out of the slot machines, and even silver dollars. Then the funnel carried the coins across the reservation and dumped them in the middle of Bad Medicine Lake. Benedictine monks, of course, were out fishing on the lake when the storm hit. Naturally, their boats were filled with coins from the casino. They realized, at that very moment, the godly message of a casino on the reservation. They were the grand winners of the tornado game.

Now, back to the serious issues of casinos. Wait, the same tornado metaphor might work in the context of sovereignty. Native sovereignty, much like the coins, could be sucked into a funnel cloud of greed and envy. The test, of course, is over the rights of reservations to operate casinos on tribal land. These are issues of native sovereignty, and legal actions by several states have raised serious legal questions about casinos. Some of these constitutional issues could be argued in the United States Supreme Court. Really, the idea of domestic or limited sovereignty could be challenged by a conservative court. How would a tribal government compete, over the question of casinos, with state sovereignty that was established in the Constitution of the United States? I fear that casinos may attract the envy and hatred of other communities.

First, let me back up a bit from casinos and point out that there is something of a radical transformation in the way people are viewing native communities these days. Every year more people gamble at indian casinos, and there are more stories about casinos on television and in newspapers. Generally speaking, more than half of all of the articles and news stories about indians in the past few years have been about casinos. Now, more than ever, the public hears or reads about indians in the context of casinos. Stories about the many programs, services supported by casino profits, political contentions, contradictions, and the neverending stories of corruption on reservations. The stories about habitual gamblers, and about organized crime, narcotics, criminal behavior, casino orphans, alcohol sales and drunken driving, and the terrible damage to families as a consequence of losing small fortunes at casinos. These issues have taken the place of many other complex issues that were once the focus of stories about native communities. Now, with that in mind, the Supreme Court could hear a casino case and rule against the idea of native sovereignty. Hannah Arendt argued in *Antisemitism* that trouble comes to people who have wealth but no power. Some natives have riches but no real power. The envy of casino riches on reservations is not a good sign for the future of native sovereignty.

ARL: Yet these casinos give native communities a particular power to bargain, as has happened in Connecticut, Minnesota, and New Mexico. Casinos also provide employment. Isn't this a real plus?

GV: Absolutely, but the native power you mention in these states is negotiated, and that power is situational at best. Treaties are semantic creations, otherwise natives would have no rights to negotiate. So the actual circumstances of native power are realized by negotiations or in court decisions, or in precedence, and in federal polices. Casinos, then, are not so much a right as a contingency of treaty or trust land. But the actual power is negotiated according to federal gaming laws. Casinos may have the cash, but even that power is based on the politics of chance.

Robert, remember that most reservations were created by treaties, and that trust is not part of the actual sovereignty granted to the states in the United States Constitution. The Indian Gaming Regulatory Act, as you know, was passed about a decade ago, and since then, reservations that plan to open casinos must negotiate a compact or some agreement with the state. So native governments were required by federal law to negotiate with states, and that seemed to reduce the very idea of native sovereignty. The keyword is *negotiate*, but that seemed to be a double cross over the gaming regulations. The federal government, once the dubious protector, has become the Janus-faced apologist for native treaty rights. One face is turned to natives and their treaties, and the other face is turned to the states and the new regulations. Native rights have never been any less complicated, but this was a new twist that several native governments refused to acknowledge. Recently, the new law tested the reality of native power and the politics of sovereignty. Florida was the first state that refused to negotiate a casino compact with a native government, the Seminoles. So the Seminole government sued the state, claiming that the state was obligated by federal law to negotiate, and that became a test of the Tenth Amendment of the Constitution. The case, on appeal, was decided in favor of the state of Florida. The Supreme Court ruled that the new federal gaming regulation was in fact unconstitutional, because states have reserved rights and cannot be sued. So you see, casinos could become the tests of manifest manners and native sovereignty.

ARL: Yet would you say that negotiations are sources of power?

GV: Yes, negotiations based on treaties, and on regulations and policies, are sources of power because many of the compacts and agreements with various states are extraordinary. Natives are negotiating with governors and state legislatures over casinos, and that, of course, is a situational power. Connecticut, for instance, has laws against casino-style gambling, but as you know, the Mashantucket Pequots negotiated an agreement with the governor to pay the state more than a hundred million dollars to operate Foxwoods Casino. Party politics and money are significant in casino negotiations, but here money has been the absolute tease of power. Casino money is situational politics, to be sure, but not the lasting power of native sovereignty.

Yes, and the party politics of situational power was the case in the state of New Mexico. The governor signed compacts with a number of pueblos to open casinos, but later, once the casinos were in operation, the legislature announced that in fact the agreement had not been ratified by the state government. So the state asked the federal attorney to close the casinos because there were no compacts according to the law. Meanwhile, native leaders told the state that if they close down the casinos the pueblos would close down the power lines and every highway that crosses native land. Now that was power, the power of resistance, but remember that the issue was situational and the state has constitutional sovereignty.

On the other hand, many reservations have massive debts, tens of millions of dollars borrowed to build these palatial casinos. Some native governments may never recover if the casinos are closed by federal or state action, or they may die a slow death by corruption. These are never easy discussions because casinos have created many new jobs in native communities, and in many states the cost of public welfare and other services has been reduced near casinos. So the point is that casinos are a source of situational money, but the power is chance, and gambling has never been a cultural answer to anything.

ARL: Two further considerations come up in connection with casinos. In the past, you've offered a critique of *The Broken Cord* by the late Michael Dorris on the grounds that it perpetuates certain stereotypes and images of the firewater myth or the Indian as perennial and irrecoverable drunk. Many now worry that casinos may provide further opportunity or occasion for the temptations of drinking and its implicit dangers. What's your take on that?

GV: You know, bingo was once a great rush, a chance to win giant prizes, and the game was a community activity. Some players covered a dozen cards and carried on conversations at the same time. Clearly, this was a case of punctuated equilibrium, or at least evidence of a native bingo gene. Yes, there were bingo orphans, but even obsessive players could not lose that much in a day. There's no denying the romance of gambling, the mythic sense of bad luck, the chance to win, but my point is that bingo and card games are more communal than casinos, and most of the bingo money goes to the players. Casino games, and especially slot machines, tease the losers, because the odds are set by the casino, and players bet against the silent house, not against the other players. Bingo and poker are shared games, in a sense, because the players bet against each other, and that is a more communal game than casino machines. Bingo and poker winners are celebrated in the presence of other players as part of the game. Casino winners are freaks because chance has been taken out of the game. So to bet against the house, in the sense of *indian* casinos, is to bet against natives. Casino machines, *indian* or not, are cheaters, and that game is nihilistic, not communal. Much worse, it seems to me, iş to cheat the obsessive losers at casinos in the native name of cultural pride, in the name of economic development, or in the virtuous name of education.

ARL: What, then, of casinos as eateries? Places of food and drink?

GV: Sovereignty, eatery, testy activity, and envy. Maybe this *indian* casino nihilism and the freak winners make more sense over the menus and buffets. Spam, baked beans, white cake, and soft drinks, for instance, were the best fare at most bingo games, but many of the new casinos have great restaurants. The first casinos served better food than bingo games, and that was a very positive change, but neither served beverage alcohol. However, the prohibition of alcohol has changed in the past few years. Now, at most *indian* casinos, gamblers can play, drink, eat, and smoke around the clock. Drinks with a meal at a casino restaurant are one thing, but service at a bar, or booze served over a slot machine, is another, and the social problems are obvious. The concern, of course, is not just alcohol, but the image of natives serving alcohol at casinos on reservations. That image is dangerous and revolutionary. Casinos and alcohol are seen by many critics as nihilistic and demonic, and in my view, the cultural tensions are terminal. Why, for instance, would natives serve liquor in a casino on Easter Sunday? Casinos that serve alcohol on religious holy days in conservative communities are sure to test the course of native sovereignty. Natives, on the one hand, ban alcohol at cultural and social events and, on the other hand, serve the same in their casinos on reservations. What is this? Greed? Vengeance?

Listen, some towns near reservations are dry, and other towns try to control the sale of alcohol in municipal stores. Casinos that serve alcohol contribute to the risk of drunken drivers on rural roads near reservations, and the increase in traffic is all the more troublesome because the cost of county or state law enforcement and road maintenance is seldom paid by native governments. Clearly, it seems to me, casinos aggravate cultural and religious conflicts in many rural communities. Remember, though, that many natives are opposed to casinos. As you know, there has been very strong, even violent opposition to casinos in several native communities. Obviously, there's much more to lose at casinos than money. Greed and envy are the heavy players at *indian* casinos, and there's more at stake than a lucky bet on roulette, or the nihilistic sound of lost coins in a slot machine. Natives might lose their tease of sovereignty.

ARL: What of the danger of organized crime in the management of reservation casinos?

GV: So, in a sense, what difference does it make if casino corruption is reservation born or from the outside? I mean, a corrupt casino is just that, no matter the direction, inside or outside. The federal government, of course, views the presence of organized criminals in the management of casinos as a serious crime, or even a conspiracy. Suppose, for instance, that some reservation casino manager is massively corrupt and hires only his friends and family, compared to an outside management company with ties to organized crime. Corruption is absolute either way, so the distinctions, apart from the nepotism, matter more to federal authorities than to ordinary natives on the reservation. The subtleties of corruption have never been easy to define on reservations, or anywhere else, for that matter. However, because of this concern over organized crime, the federal government now requires that managers of casinos undergo a background investigation. Native governments are elected on many reservations, and in some cases, the elected representatives assume the management of the casinos. That, obviously, has created problems of accountability. Maybe casino managers should run in separate elections on reservations.

ARL: You were once a journalist. In that context, what, in general, about the media coverage of issues like reservation casinos?

GV: Compared to the general news stories a generation ago and earlier, the reports about natives today are superior. Journalists have much more experience with the cultural and legal complexities of native communities, and they probably come to their profession with a better general education about natives, the history of treaties, and reservations. I mean, journalists are much more sensitive to racial and cultural categories. News reports and feature stories about natural resources, about the development of reservation resources, about casinos, about education, about federal lawsuits, about native water rights, and about criminal justice are much more informed and articulate, for the most part, on the real issues that engage natives today. Obviously, most native issues are very complex because of treaties and community differences, and journalists must find a way to state native issues more simply. Sometimes native issues are reduced to romantic notions and collective *indian* simulations, and sometimes natives themselves present their issues in that way. And that, of course, is usually at the expense of the subtleties and contradictions that give natives a rich and complex history. There is still a tendency to reduce issues to a binary structure, such as the familiar theme of savagism and civilization, and the reversal of that theme, and so many reports focus on the government as evil and natives as the victims. That, of course, is not the case in native politics. Natives are politically shrewd, and their legal arguments are not the romance of victimry. Even so, the mighty politics of casinos has dominated, more than any other single issue, most of the news stories about natives in the past decade. Casinos are big money, and big money is political, and money and politics are situational power. Newspapers pay attention to the power players.

ARL: We've spoken about the problems of native studies programs and departments. But do you get the sense that native culture is being offered sufficiently in the public school curriculum? Are more texts being read? Are more histories being learned?

GV: There is more information about *indians* in public schools, to be sure, but much of that is a simulation based on movies, the romantic politics of the other in popular culture, and the usual scientific sources. Yes, and natives have provided or sanctioned much of this material in public schools. Natives, or simulated *indians*, are presented as an absence in the curriculum, more as a minority group, a culture of disadvantage and victimry. Natives, in other words, are seldom presented as a presence of diverse individuals, cultures, and communities. And only recently has there been much attention to the reality, or the obvious presence, of crossblood natives in public schools.

But how and who should critique the value of this material about natives in the public schools? How much of a culture dare a teacher reduce and simplify? Should natives be the only arbiters of such course materials, or do natives create their own romantic and essentialist histories? How are natives presented in the context of national history? Separate, as an *indian* absence, or as an active presence in the creases of national histories? Maybe a good example is the estimate, or underestimation, of indigenous populations. Most public school history texts, at least until the past decade or so, have recorded a total population of about half a million natives on the continent at the time of Christopher Columbus. This has understated the presence of natives by the millions and, it seems to me, leaves students with the impression that indigenous cultures were not that significant, and so the colonial displacement of only a half million people on such a vast continent is not that much of a problem. Clearly this is a reductive history of victimry. That, of course, is not the case.

Many demographic studies have pointed out that the population of natives on the continent was much greater than a million. Henry Dobyns, for instance, has developed a depopulation ratio theory to estimate the number of natives on the continent in the fifteenth century, or before Columbus. He based his theory on the rate of death by diseases, and natives at the time had no known immunities to the lethal pathogens that were brought by traders and colonists. Dobyns estimated that with a given rate of death by diseases there might have been ten million natives in North America, thirty million in what is now Mexico and Central America, and an estimated population of sixty million in South America. The total, then, based on a depopulation ratio, or how many natives there might have been based on later studies and enumerations, was estimated to be about one hundred million in the hemisphere. There are many ways to study native populations, but the depopulation ratio seems to be more comprehensible.

European settlement, teachers might explain, displaced only about a million natives, and that would be a double tragedy. The first tragedy was colonialism and disease, and the second tragedy is the reduction of native populations in history. The depopulation estimates are seldom if ever discussed in public schools. American history, based on these new theories of an estimated one hundred million natives, could not be told in the same way.

ARL: Following your first year as a college teacher you worked in a public school near the White Earth Reservation in Minnesota. What were your experiences there, and is that where you formed some of your critical ideas about education?

GV: The *Minneapolis Tribune* granted me a one-year leave to teach at Lake Forest College in Illinois. That was my first experience as a college teacher, and it was possible only because of the trust and good humor of Jerry Gerasimo and George Mills. They were both on the faculty in the social sciences and invited me to create my own courses about Native Americans. Mills was a brilliant teacher, a mighty mediator of irony, and in his range of reason and generous humor the world became an exciting contradiction. He was chair of the department and hired me not because of my knowledge of the social sciences but, he said over dinner, because of my haiku poetry. Yes, he was a haiku poet and thought such understated acts of imagistic creation were far more significant to the world than bean counts or comparative measures of culture. My first courses were tricky conversions of haiku reason and, in that sense, visionary spread sheets of native stories.

I might have stayed a second year, but the plague of recreational drugs among privileged students was very discouraging, and at the same time, my friends in native education convinced me to take a position as director of a federal desegregation program in the Park Rapids School District, near the White Earth Reservation in northern Minnesota. This program was funded by the federal government because the dropout rate among natives was over 90 percent, and that in a consolidated school east of the reservation was described as segregation. I worked with the school board, the administrators, teachers, bus drivers, and the maintenance staff to reverse the conditions that caused so many bright natives to leave school before graduation. This would not have been a school for me either, so my job was a real challenge.

I started by reviewing the school records of native students who should have graduated in the past two years. These students had attended the elementary school at Pine Point on the White Earth Reservation, and then in the eighth grade they were bused to and from the consolidated school about twenty miles away in Park Rapids. Overall the native students did very well in the elementary school on the reservation, but most of them failed in the first or second year in high school. In fact, as a group, these students who dropped out had earned high grades and scored about one year above national norms on standard tests. That these students had scored so high on standard tests surprised everyone, including me, because most of us who had been active in native education at the time accepted the view that many reservation children had a cultural disadvantage on standardized achievement tests.

The White Earth Reservation was an exception, we tried to reason, but at last we understood the simple reality of the test results. The good teachers in the elementary school on the reservation loved their students and convinced them to do their very best, and they did just that. They did their best year after year, until they entered the Park Rapids School. There, in the first year, these same bright students scored one year below national norms on standard tests. My job became all the more difficult with this information because the teachers, who were good people, could not accept the fact that native students had scored so high on standard tests. Most of the teachers were convinced that these same students were not capable of abstract thought or reason because they were culturally deprived *indians*, and because many of them were from complicated families on the reservation. The teachers were sympathetic, but by no means capable, at the time, of understanding manifest manners and the failure of their own public school. By "cultural deprivation" most of the teachers meant the absence of books, magazines, and television in the home. The teachers were wrong, of course, but there was no real chance to convince them otherwise. Clearly, these teachers were not prepared to accept the obvious conclusion that native students were not the cause of scholastic segregation.

The Park Rapids Schools badly served these native students, and the best those students could do was leave a system of shame and victimry. Otherwise, these bright, enthusiastic students would be turned into deprived cultural objects. In my view, their response to the public school was not so much a failure as an act of courage and survivance. Actually, my advice to other students was to leave a system that refused to honor their presence. This, of course, was a wild irony because my duties were to find a way to reverse segregation in the school district, and that meant to increase the number of native graduates. My advise to students was to leave, to act with courage, and to rise above the mundane racialism of the school and teachers. I encouraged those students who had already abandoned the system to complete high school in a general education program on the reservation. Many students did just that, and several of these same students went on to college. The general education programs were more mature and supportive of natives. My mission, in a sense, was native survivance.

Obviously, the few native students who rode the bus and were in school every morning, and determined to graduate, deserved my support more than anyone at the time. They were wise about the situation, and we discussed the reasons why they, but not others, continued to attend the public school at Park Rapids. Why did you stay? My rhetorical question placed the burden on staying, not leaving. There was no shame in leaving a school that did not support natives. Well, the answer for most native students was quite easy. They were close to at least one teacher, or they were involved in special activities, arts performances, or athletics, and their presence was important to the school. The students said that the teachers who expressed an active, personal interest in them made all the difference in the world. One of the obvious problems was that natives were bused to the school from the reservation and were not part of the community. Other students who were bused from rural farms told me about their sense of separation from the students in town. Personal attention, of course, makes a difference in any community. No one needs a federal program to figure that much out.

Even so, the high scores by native students on the national tests were a great discovery. My view of native education has never been the same since. That simple reality – community support, very strict and supportive teachers who want their students to achieve, and maybe a nutritious breakfast – can change the situations of education. Cultural deprivation does not explain anything, because there are natives and other students who experience poverty and adversity, and yet many of them are creative, witty, and very good students.

ARL: And yet, in the last two, three decades, since you directed that program, the cry has been multiculturalism. The cry has been diversity. The cry has been identity politics. Now a strong countermovement of conservatives in education, politics, and government have taken their lead from, say, Allan Bloom, William Bennett, Lynne Cheney. Where does native studies, where does native education, stand in that debate?

GV: Robert, natives are the natural tease of education on this continent, and that means a visionary presence and a reciprocity with nature, but these thumbnail debates over culture and the nostalgic revisions of a conservative paradise are no better than the pretense and treacheries of the early pilgrim separatists. Native stories, and a native presence, are the obvious start of histories on this continent. Natives created the diversity of the continent, and any studies of this country must start with the cultures of Native Americans.

Natives created their diverse presence on this continent as a visionary sovereignty. More than an estimated forty million natives on this continent lived in a reciprocal union with nature for several thousand years. That union is the originary story of the place. Long before the eager explorers and colonial settlement, natives hunted, farmed, and built extensive irrigation systems. Long before the fur trade, native hunters honored the animals. Long before the Spanish Empire, natives had established elaborate trade routes on the continent. Long before the British Empire, natives cleared land for gardens and created animal and bird habitats. Long before treaties with the United States, natives had established ceremonial connections and political associations with other cultures. Long before Richard Pratt, natives were educated in the stories of their survivance. Long before the American Indian Movement, natives defeated the Spanish Empire. First, this is a diverse native continent.

That history is not celebrated very often in public school texts or classrooms. Mostly, *indians* are presented as simulations in concise cultural dioramas. And yet, of course, natives are the very start of any history of the United States. Not the absence of natives, not the myths of savagism and civilization, not mere museum natives, and not natives as eternal victims, but natives as a diverse continental presence. The history of this country is a native reciprocity with nature, and that visionary, biocentric connection to the environment is what saved most of the early settlers and separatists from starvation. Allan Bloom, and many other modern separatists, might have learned a wiser tune of survivance in native communities. Lynne Cheney and the conservatives trump their own simulations of civilization. Natives continue to be the diverse storiers of this continent, not the separatists.

ARL: Therefore, any accounting of America that offers itself as multicultural has a root-and-branch obligation to recognize native history and culture most of all, a set of voices that too often, would you say, has been missing from the overall account of what passes as American culture?

GV: Yes, to recognize the presence of natives means that natives are the start of any national or continental history. Natives are the first diverse cultures of this continent, but that obvious fact is ignored by conservative separatists and revised by every stripe of missionary, cultist, romantic, fanatic, ideologue, and even some ethnic studies scholars. Natives, yes, many native cultures, carried out the very first affirmative action programs in this country. The first separatists were trouble, and they have always been trouble. Natives first carried out these multicultural actions with other natives and diverse cultures, and that generous practice has continued since the separatists settled on the continent. Explorers and early settlers have acknowledged that natives were not the separatists. Native resistance is survivance, not separatism, and many natives continue to resist the racialists and separatists.

Natives have resisted the colonial separatists at every river, at every mountain, at every treeline, at every lake; and in every treaty natives have carried on their resistance in the company of animals, birds, tricksters, and visionary sovereignty. The separatists were treacherous, but natives have resisted their manifest manners and dominance. The separatists have tried to ruin nature, and even the memories of native survivance, but most natives resist the romance of victimry. This is a diverse native country, not a separatist nation.

ARL: You started your career in journalism and education more than thirty years ago. What has become of multicultural programs at universities in the past decade? What is the future of native or ethnic studies?

GV: You might expect natives to find some solace for their visions, originary stories, and resistance to empire at universities and in ethnic studies departments, but that has not been the case in my experience. Regrettably, many natives have encountered anew the separatists in academic robes, and some of these ethnic separatists are in administrative positions. Natives, more often than not, are caught in the ethnic contests over budgets and academic positions and waived aside in the national ideologies of Asians and Chicanos. Natives are not the new immigrants, not the separatists, and not the ethnic simulations of cultural victimry. Natives are the diverse visionary sovereigns of this continent.

ARL: Gerald, there could be no better close to our conversations. We started with your tease of humor and memory. We close with your vision of native sovereignty. Just shows what happens when you get talking with Britishers who teach American studies.

Selected References

◆ Books Written by Gerald Vizenor

Fugitive Poses: Native American Indian Scenes of Absence and Presence. Lincoln: Univ. of Nebraska Press, 1998.

Hotline Healers: An Almost Browne Novel. Hanover NH: Wesleyan Univ. Press, Univ. Press of New England, 1997.

Manifest Manners: Postindian Warriors of Survivance. Hanover NH: Wesleyan Univ. Press, Univ. Press of New England, 1994.

Shadow Distance: A Gerald Vizenor Reader. Ed. A. Robert Lee. Hanover NH: Wesleyan Univ. Press, Univ. Press of New England, 1994.

Harold of Orange/Harold Von Orangen. Trans. Wolfgang Hochbruck. Eggingen, Germany: Editions Klaus Isele, 1994.

Dead Voices: Natural Agonies in the New World. Norman: Univ. of Oklahoma Press, 1992.

The Heirs of Columbus. Hanover NH: Wesleyan Univ. Press, Univ. Press of New England, 1991; paperbound edition 1992.

Landfill Meditation. Hanover NH: Wesleyan Univ. Press, Univ. Press of New England, 1991.

Interior Landscapes: Autobiographical Myths and Metaphors. Minneapolis: Univ. of Minnesota Press, 1990.

Crossbloods: Bone Courts, Bingo, and Other Reports. Minneapolis: Univ. of Minnesota Press, 1990.

Griever: An American Monkey King in China. Normal: Illinois State University, Fiction Collective, 1987. Reprint. Univ. of Minnesota Press, 1990. Fiction Collective Award, New York, 1986. American Book Award, 1988.

Bearheart: The Heirship Chronicles. Revised edition. Minneapolis: Univ. of Minnesota Press, 1990. First published as *Darkness in Saint Louis Bearheart.* St. Paul MN: Truck Press, 1978.

The Trickster of Liberty: Tribal Heirs to a Wild Baronage. Minneapolis: Univ. of Minnesota Press, 1988.

Matsushima: Pine Islands. Minneapolis: Nodin Press, 1984.

The People Named the Chippewa: Narrative Histories. Minneapolis: Univ. of Minnesota Press, 1983.

Earthdivers: Tribal Narratives on Mixed Descent. Minneapolis: Univ. of Minnesota Press, 1983.

Wordarrows: Indians and Whites in the New Fur Trade. Minneapolis: Univ. of Minnesota Press, 1978. Italian translation: *Parolefrecce.* Trans. Maria Vittoria D'Amico. Pisa: Univ. of Pisa, 1992.

The Everlasting Sky: New Voices from the People Named the Chippewa. New York: Crowell-Collier, 1972.

Thomas James White Hawk, Mound MN: Four Winds Press, 1968.

◆ Books Edited by Gerald Vizenor

Native American Literature. New York: HarperCollins, 1995.

Narrative Chance: Postmodern Discourse on Native American Literatures. With an introduction and an essay, "Trickster Discourse." Albuquerque: Univ. of New Mexico Press, 1989. Paperbound edition, Norman: Univ. of Oklahoma Press, 1993.

Touchwood: A Collection of Ojibwe Prose. With an introduction and two stories. Saint Paul MN: New Rivers Press, 1987.

Summer in the Spring: Ojibwe Lyric Poems and Tribal Stories. St. Paul MN: Nodin Press, 1981. Revised edition. *Summer in the Spring: Anishinaabe Lyric Poems and Stories.* Norman: Univ. of Oklahoma Press, 1993.

◆ Short Fiction, Poetry, and Published Excerpts from Longer Works by Gerald Vizenor

"Feral Lasers." *Caliban* 6 (1989): 16–23. Reprint in *Postmodern American Fiction: A Norton Anthology,* ed. Paula Geyh, Fred Leebron, and Andrew Levy. New York: Norton, 1998.

"Oshkiwiinag: Heartlines on the Trickster Express." In *The Year's Best Fantasy and Horror,* 10th annual collection, ed. Ellen Datlow and Terri Windling. New York: St. Martin's Press, 1997. Also published in *Blue*

Dawn, Red Earth, ed. Clifford Trafzer. Garden City NY: Anchor Books, 1996. First published in *Religion and Literature* 26 (spring 1994): 142–57.

"Hotline Healers: Virtual Animals on Panda Radio." *Caliban* 15 (1995): 16–28.

"Stone Columbus: Talk Radio from the Santa Maria Casino." In *After Yesterday's Crash: The Avant-Pop Anthology*, ed. Larry McCaffery. New York: Viking Penguin, 1995.

"Monte Cassino Curiosa: Heart Dancers at the Headwaters." *Caliban* 14 (1994): 60–70.

"Almost Browne." In *The Harper American Literature*, ed. Donald Mc-Quade. New York: HarperCollins, 1994.

"The Moccasin Game." In *Earth Songs, Sky Spirit*, ed. Clifford Trafzer. Garden City, NY: Doubleday, 1993.

"Reversal of Fortunes: Tribalism in the Nick of Time." *Caliban* 13 (1993): 22–28. Reprinted in *Shadow Distance*, 1994.

"Wingo on the Santa Maria." In *Avante-Pop: Fiction for a Daydream Nation*, ed. Larry McCaffery. Boulder CO: Black Ice Books, 1993.

"Our Land: Anishinaabe." *Native Peoples Magazine*, spring 1993.

"Wortlichtspiele." Scenes from *Harold of Orange* in German trans. *Chelsea Hotel* 2 (Eggingen, Germany, 1992).

"Sturmpuppen." The chapter "Storm Puppets" from *The Heirs of Columbus* in German trans. *Chelsea Hotel* 1 (Eggingen, Germany, 1992).

"Bound Feet" and "Holosexual Clown." From *Griever: An American Monkey King in China*. In *The Before Columbus Foundation Fiction Anthology*. New York: Norton, 1992.

"Moccasin Games." In *Without Discovery*, ed. Ray Gonzales. Seattle: Broken Moon Press, 1992. Earlier version published in *Caliban* 9 (1990): 96–109.

"The Baron of Patronia" and "China Browne." In *Talking Leaves: Contemporary American Short Stories*, ed. Craig Lesley. New York: Dell, Laurel Paperback, 1991.

"Luminous Thighs." In *The Lightning Within*, ed. Alan Velie. Norman: Univ. of Oklahoma Press, 1991.

"The Last Lecture." In *American Indian Literature*, ed. Alan Velie. Norman: Univ. of Oklahoma Press, 1991.

"The Stone Trickster." *Northeast Indian Quarterly* 8 (fall 1991): 26–27.

"The Heirs of Columbus." Selected stories. *Fiction International* 20 (fall 1991): 182–92.

"An Introduction to Haiku." 16 poems and a critical introduction. *Neeuropa* (summer 1991, spring 1992): 63–67.

"Four Skin." *Tamaqua* 2 (winter 1991): 89–104.

"Almost a Whole Trickster." In *A Gathering of Flowers*, ed. Joyce Carol Thomas. New York: Harper and Row, 1990.

"Almost Browne: The Twice Told Tribal Trickster." PEN Syndicated Fiction Project, 1990. Newspaper and radio distribution and publication in *American Short Fiction*, Austin: Univ. of Texas Press.

"Water Striders." Haiku. Santa Cruz CA: Moving Parts Press, 1989.

"The Pink Flamingos." *Caliban* 7 (1989): 140–49.

"Bad Breath." In *An Illuminated History of the Future*, ed. Curtis White. Normal: Illinois State Univ., Fiction Collective Two, 1989.

L'arbe à paroles: 14 poètes amérindiens contemporains. 7 poems in French trans. by Manuel Van Thienen. *Identités wallonie* 65, special issue (Brussels, autumn 1989): 122–25.

"White Earth" and four other poems. In *Harper's Anthology of Twentieth-Century Native American Poetry*, ed. Duane Niatum. New York: Harper & Row, 1988.

"Bound Feet." *Fiction International* 17 (spring 1987): 4–8.

"Episodes in Mythic Verism: Monsignor Missalwait's Interstate." In *The New Native American Novel: Works in Progress*, ed. Mary Dougherty Bartlett. Albuquerque: Univ. of New Mexico Press, 1986.

"Reservation Café: The Origin of American Indian Instant Coffee." In *Earth Power Coming*, ed. Simon Ortiz. Tsaile AZ: Navajo Community College Press, 1983. French trans.: "Café réserve, ou Les origins du café instanté," trans. Manuel Van Thienen, in *Sur le dos de la tortue, revue bilingue de littérature amerindienne*, 1991.

Bearheart, selections. In *Stand in Good Relations to the Earth,* trans. and ed. Alexandre Vaschenko. Moscow: Raduga, 1983.

Several poems. In *American Indian Poets,* trans. and ed. Alexandre Vaschenko. Moscow: Raduga, 1983.

"Four Haiku Poems." German trans. in *Geflüsterte Pfeile.* Karlsruhe: Von Loeper Verlag, 1982.

"Paraday at the Berkeley Chicken Center." *Metropolis Magazine,* Minneapolis, April 12, 1977. Revised version as "Paraday Chicken Pluck" in *Earthdivers: Tribal Narratives on Mixed Descent.* Minneapolis: Univ. of Minnesota Press, 1981.

◆ Essays by Gerald Vizenor

"Transethnic Anthropologism." In *Margins in British and American Literature, Film, and Culture,* ed. Marita Nadal and Dolores Herreto. Zaragoza, Spain: Department de Filologia Inglesa y Alemana, Universidad de Zaragoza, 1997.

"Postindian Autoinscriptions: The Origins of Essentialism and Pluralism in Descriptive Tribal Names." In *Cultural Difference and the Literary Text,* ed. Winfried Siemerling and Katrin Schwenk. Iowa City: Univ. of Iowa Press, 1996.

"Bone Courts: The Rights and Narrative Representations of Tribal Bones." *American Indian Quarterly* 10 (1986): 319–31. Reprinted and revised as "Bone Courts: The Natural Rights of Tribal Remains" in *The Interrupted Life.* New York: Museum of Contemporary Art, 1991. Reprinted in *Contemporary Archaeology in Theory,* ed. Robert Preucel and Ian Hodder. Oxford: Blackwell, 1996.

"Gambling." In *Encyclopedia of North American Indians,* ed. Frederick Hoxie. Boston: Houghton Mifflin, 1996.

"Indian Identities." In *A Companion to American Thought,* ed. Richard Wightman Fox and James Kloppenberg. Oxford: Blackwell, 1995.

"Authored Animals: Creature Tropes in Native American Fiction." In *Social Research* 62 (1995): 661–83.

"Visions, Scares, and Stories." In *Contemporary Authors* 22 (1995): 255–77.

"Native American Indian Identities: Autoinscriptions and the Cultures of Names." *Genre: Forms of Discourse and Culture* 25 (1992): 431–40.

Reprinted in *Native American Perspectives on Literature and History*, ed. Alan Velie. Norman: Univ. of Oklahoma Press, 1995.

"Gerald Vizenor." *Zyzzyva* 32 (winter 1992): 126–43. Reprinted in *The Writer's Notebook*, ed. Howard Junker. New York: HarperCollins, 1995.

"The Ruins of Representation: Shadow Survivance and the Literature of Dominance." *American Indian Quarterly* 17 (1993): 7–30. Reprinted in *An Other Tongue*, ed. Alfred Arteaga. Durham NC: Duke Univ. Press, 1994.

"The Envoy to Haiku." *Chicago Review* 39 (1993): 55–62.

"The Tragic Wisdom of Salamanders." *Caliban* 12 (1993): 16–27. Reprinted in *Sacred Trusts: Essays on Stewardship and Responsibility*, ed. Michael Katakis. San Francisco: Mercury House, 1993.

"Krahen auf die Pappeln geschrieben." German trans. by Mabel Lesch. *Chelsea Hotel* 3 (1993): 46–50.

"Gambling on Sovereignty." *American Indian Quarterly* 16 (summer 1992): 411–13. Reprinted in *Japan Times Weekly*, Tokyo, August 1993.

"Manifest Manners: The Long Gaze of Christopher Columbus." *Boundary* 2 (1993): 223–35.

"Trickster Photography: Simulations in the Ethnographic Present." *Exposure* 29 (fall 1993): 4–5.

"Many Point Camp." In *Inheriting the Land*, ed. Mark Vinz and Thom Tammaro. Minneapolis: Univ. of Minnesota Press, 1993.

"Ishi Bares His Chest: Tribal Simulations and Survivance." In *Partial Recall: Photographs of Native North Americans*, ed. Lucy Lippard. New York: New Press, 1992.

"Native American Indian Literature: Critical Metaphors of the Ghost Dance." *World Literature Today* 66 (spring 1992): 223–27.

"Confrontation or Negotiation." In *Native American Testimony*, ed. Peter Nabokov. New York: Viking Penguin, 1991.

"Socioacupuncture: Mythic Reversals and the Striptease in Four Scenes." In *The American Indian and Problems of History*, ed. Calvin Martin. New York: Oxford Univ. Press, 1987. Reprinted in *Out There: Marginalization and Contemporary Cultures*. Cambridge MA: MIT Press; New York: New Museum of Contemporary Art, 1990.

"Postmodern Discourse on Native American Literature." *Halcyon* 12 (1990): 43–48.

"Native American Dissolve." *Oshkaabewis Native Journal* 1 (1990): 63–65.

"Trickster Discourse." *Wicazo Sa Review* 5 (spring 1989): 2–7.

"Wampum to Pictures of Presidents." In *From Different Shores: Perspectives on Race and Ethnicity in America*, ed. Ronald Takaki. New York: Oxford Univ. Press, 1987.

"Crows Written on the Poplars: Autocritical Autobiographies." In *I Tell You Now: Autobiographical Essays by Native American Writers*, ed. Arnold Krupat. Lincoln: Univ. of Nebraska Press, 1987.

"I Know What You Mean, Erdupps MacChurbbs: Autobiographical Myths and Metaphors." In *Growing Up in Minnesota: Ten Writers Remember Their Childhoods*, ed. Chester Anderson. Minneapolis: Univ. of Minnesota Press, 1976.

◆ Selected Interviews

"Postindian Comments: Gerald Vizenor in Dialogue with A. Robert Lee." *Third Text* 43 (summer 1998): 1–11.

"On Thin Ice, You Might as Well Dance." In Larry McCaffery, *Some Other Frequency: Interviews with Innovative American Authors*. Philadelphia: Univ. of Pennsylvania Press, 1996.

"Gerald Vizenor." Interview by Helmbrecht Breinig and Klaus Lösch in *American Contradictions: Interviews with Nine American Writers*, ed. Wolfgang Binder and Helmbrecht Breinig. Hanover NH: Wesleyan Univ. Press, Univ. Press of New England, 1995.

"Mythic Rage and Laughter: An Interview with Gerald Vizenor." By Dallas Miller. *Studies in American Indian Literatures* 7, no.1 (spring 1995): 77–96.

"Head Water: An Interview with Gerald Vizenor." By Larry McCaffery and Tom Marshall. *Chicago Review* 39 (1993): 50–54.

" 'I Defy Analysis': A Conversation with Gerald Vizenor." By Rodney Simard. *Studies in American Indian Literatures* 5 (fall 1993): 43–51.

"Gerald Vizenor." In *Winged Words: American Indian Writers Speak*, ed. Laura Coltelli. Lincoln: Univ. of Nebraska Press, 1990.

"Follow the Trickroutes: An Interview with Gerald Vizenor." In *Survival*

This Way: Interviews with American Indian Poets, ed. Joseph Bruchac. Tucson: Univ. of Arizona Press, 1987.

"An Interview with Gerald Vizenor." By Neal Bowers and Charles Silet. Melus 8, no.1 (1981) 41–49.

◆ Selected Critical Studies:

Owens, Louis. " 'Grinning Aboriginal Demons': Gerald Vizenor's Bearheart and the End of Tragedy." In Mixedblood Messages. Norman: Univ. of Oklahoma Press, 1998.

Lee, A. Robert. "Towards America's Ethnic Postmodern: The Novels of Ishmael Reed, Maxine Hong Kingston, Ana Castillo, and Gerald Vizenor." In Contemporary Fiction and Cultural Identity in North America, ed. Jaap Lindvelt, Richard Saint-Gelais, W. M. Verhoeven, and Catherine Raffi-Béroud. Quebec: Editions Nota Bene, 1998.

Helstern, Linda Lizut. "Blue Smoke and Mirrors: Griever's Buddhist Heart." One of eight essays on Gerald Vizenor in a special edition of Studies in American Indian Literatures, ed. Louis Owens, vol.9, no.1 (spring 1997): 33–46.

Weaver, Jace. "Gerald Vizenor." In That the People Might Live: Native American Literatures and Native American Community. New York: Oxford Univ. Press, 1997.

Seesequasis, Paul. "Trick or Treat? What Kind of Indian are You?" In Why Are You Telling Me This? Eleven Acts of Intimate Journalism, ed. Heather Elton, Barbara Moon, and Don Obe. Banff AB: Banff Center Press, 1997.

Blaeser, Kimberly. Gerald Vizenor: Writing in the Oral Tradition. Norman: Univ. of Oklahoma Press, 1996.

Krupat, Arnold. "Ratio- and Natio- in Gerald Vizenor's Heirs of Columbus." In The Turn to the Native. Lincoln: Univ. of Nebraska Press, 1996.

Ruppert, James. "Mythic Verism: Bearheart: The Heirship Chronicles." In Mediation in Contemporary Native American Fiction. Norman: Univ. of Oklahoma Press, 1995.

Rodriguez, Juana Maria. "Vizenor's Shadow Plays: Mediations and Multiplicities of Power." In Native American Perspectives on Literature and History, ed. Alan Velie. Norman: Univ. of Oklahoma Press, 1995.

Lee, A. Robert. Introduction. In Shadow Distance: A Gerald Vizenor Reader.

Hanover NH: Wesleyan Univ. Press, Univ. Press of New England, 1994.

Lee, A. Robert. "Afro-America, the Before Columbus Foundation, and the Literary Multiculturalization of America." *Journal of American Studies* 28, no.3 (December 1994).

Blaeser, Kimberly. "The Multiple Traditions of Gerald Vizenor's Haiku Poetry." In *New Voices in Native American Literary Criticism*, ed. Arnold Krupat. Washington DC: Smithsonian Institution Press, 1993.

Sims, Cecilia. "The Rebirth of Indian and Chinese Mythology in Gerald Vizenor's *Griever: An American Monkey King in China*." In *Critical Perspectives on Native American Fiction*, ed. Richard Fleck. Washington DC: Three Continents Press, 1993.

Linton, Patricia. "The 'Person' in Postmodern Fiction: Gibson, Le Guin, and Vizenor." One of five essays on Gerald Vizenor in a special issue of *Studies in American Indian Literatures*, ed. Rodney Simard, vol.5, no.3 (fall 1993): 3–11.

Lee, A. Robert. "Self-Inscriptions: James Baldwin, Tomás Riversa, Gerald Vizenor, and Amy Tan and the Writing-in of America's Non-European Ethnicities." In *A Permanent Etcetera: Cross-Cultural Perspectives on Post-War America*, ed. A. Robert Lee. London: Pluto Press; Boulder CO: Westview Press, 1993.

Louis Owens. "Ecstatic Strategies: Gerald Vizenor's Trickster Narratives." In *Other Destinies: Understanding the American Indian Novel*. Norman: Univ. of Oklahoma Press, 1992.

Boyarin, Jonathan. "Europe's Indian, America's Jew: Modiano and Vizenor." In *Storm from Paradise*. Minneapolis: Univ. of Minnesota Press, 1992.

Ruoff, A. LaVonne Brown. "Woodland Word Warrior: An Introduction to Gerald Vizenor with a Bibliography of His Work." *Melus* 13, nos.1–2 (spring–summer 1986): 13–43.

Ruoff, A. LaVonne Brown. "Gerald Vizenor: Compassionate Trickster." One of seven essays on Gerald Vizenor in a special edition of *American Indian Quarterly*, ed. Terry Wilson, vol.9, no.1 (winter 1985): 67–73.

Velie, Alan. "Beyond the Novel Chippewa-style: Gerald Vizenor's Post-Modern Fiction." In *Four American Indian Literary Masters*. Norman: Univ. of Oklahoma Press, 1982.